Financial Terms Dictionary

Principles of Economics Explained

Published July 01, 2017

Revision 1.1

Financial Terms Dictionary

Copyright And Trademark Notices

Limits of Liability and Disclaimer of Warranties

The materials in this book are provided "as is" and without warranties of any kind either express or implied. The Author disclaims all warranties, express or implied, including, but not limited to, implied warranties of merchantability and fitness for a particular purpose.

The Author does not warrant that defects will be corrected, or that that the site or the server that makes this eBook available are free of viruses or other harmful components. The Author does not warrant or make any representations regarding the use or the results of the use of the materials in this book in terms of their correctness, accuracy, reliability, or otherwise. Applicable law may not allow the exclusion of implied warranties, so the above exclusion may not apply to you.

Under no circumstances, including, but not limited to, negligence, shall the Author be liable for any special or consequential damages that result from the use of, or the inability to use this eBook, even if the Author or his authorised representative has been advised of the possibility of such damages.

Applicable law may not allow the limitation or exclusion of liability or incidental or consequential damages, so the above limitation or exclusion may not apply to you. In no event shall the Author's total liability to you for all damages, losses, and causes of action (whether in contract, tort, including but not limited to, negligence or otherwise) exceed the amount paid by you, if any, for this eBook.

Facts and information are believed to be accurate at the time they were placed in this book. All data provided in this book is to be used for information purposes only. The information contained within is not intended to provide specific legal, financial or tax advice, or any other advice whatsoever, for any individual or company and should not be relied upon in that regard. The services described are only offered in jurisdictions where they may be legally offered. Information provided is not all-inclusive, and is limited to information that is made available and such information should not be relied upon as all-inclusive or accurate.

About the Author

Thomas Herold is a successful entrepreneur and personal development coach. After a career with one of the largest electronic companies in the world, he realised that a regular job would never fully satisfy his need for connection on a deep level. The only way to live his full potential was to start building his own business and find new ways to be in service to others.

For over 25 years he has helped many people - including himself - build their dream businesses. Toward that goal, he focuses on education, simplified and enhanced by modern technology. He is the author of 15 books with over 200,000 copies distributed worldwide.

Other than his passion for creating businesses, Thomas has spent over 20 years in the self-development field. Placing emphasis on the exploration of consciousness and building practical applications that allow people to express their purpose and passion in life, Thomas's work in this area has provided ample and happy proof that this approach works.

He believes that every person has at least one gift and that, when this gift is developed and nourished, it will serve as a fountainhead of personal happiness and help contribute to a better, more sustainable world.

For the past twelve years Thomas has studied the monetary system and has experienced some profound insights on how money and wealth are related. He has recently committed to sharing this financial knowledge in a new venture - the Financial Terms Dictionary, a hub of financial term descriptions designed to help people get started on their own money makeover and get a financial education in the process.

Thomas's ultimate vision for the Financial Terms Dictionary is to empower people to adopt a wealthy mindset and to create abundance for themselves and others. His ability to explain complex information in simple terms makes him an outstanding teacher and coach.

For more information please visit: Financial Terms Dictionary

Financial Dictionary Series

There are 12 books in this financial dictionaries series available. Click the links below to see an overview and available formats. There is also a premium edition available, which covers over 900 financial terms!

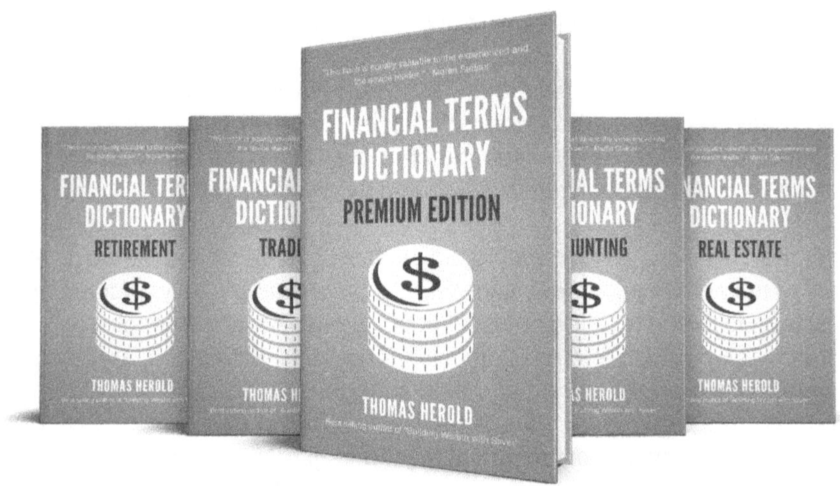

Standard Editions
Financial Terms Dictionary - Accounting Edition
Financial Terms Dictionary - Banking Edition
Financial Terms Dictionary - Corporate Finance Edition
Financial Terms Dictionary - Economics Edition
Financial Terms Dictionary - Investment Edition
Financial Terms Dictionary - Laws & Regulations Edition
Financial Terms Dictionary - Real Estate Edition
Financial Terms Dictionary - Retirement Edition
Financial Terms Dictionary - Trading Edition
Financial Terms Dictionary - Acronyms Edition

Basic & Premium Editions
Financial Terms Dictionary - Basic Edition
Financial Terms Dictionary - Premium Edition

Table Of Contents

Adam Smith

Adam Smith wrote the economic and political world shaking book *The Wealth of Nations*. This book marked the original birth of free market economics. It also spelled the doom of mercantilism, the dominant economic system of the day.

March 9, 1776 marked the publication of *An Inquiry into the Nature and Causes of the Wealth of Nations* that became known by the shorter title *The Wealth of Nations* around the world. Smith opposed mercantilism that predominated in the world economy of his day. Mercantilism believed that the amount of global wealth was limited and fixed.

The only way for countries to increase in prosperity lay in stockpiling gold and protecting markets from competition using tariffs. At the time nations felt they should sell their goods to others but not purchase any of their trade partners' goods back. This caused international trade to be extremely limited because of the trade wars and tariffs that constantly erupted.

The central part of Adam Smith's premise lay in the "invisible hand." He argued that mankind acted in his own best interests naturally. This would result in prosperity because the invisible hand of free markets would ensure the optimal economic production levels. Smith wanted all individuals to be allowed to make and exchange the goods they wished in free trade.

He believed that all markets around the world would function better if allowed to freely compete. A national government would not need to intervene much except to support the invisible hand and its magic. He promoted the idea that countries could achieve universal prosperity if they had the three elements of enlightened self interest, free market economy with strong currency, and limited government.

Smith believed that individuals should labor in their self interest with hard work and thriftiness. He believed in an enlightened form of self interest as the natural trait for most people.

His famous example surrounded a butcher who supplied meat. He did not do it out of a good heart. The butcher sold the meat to profit. By selling low quality meat he would lose customers and not make any profits. The butcher's best interests lay in offering quality meat to his customers at a fair price. Both groups realized a benefit with each transaction. Smith said that long term thinking would stop the majority of businesses from cheating their clientele. The government would enforce laws and penalties for those that failed.

This self interest extended to trade. Individuals who saved would invest for better returns and give industry the investment capital it needed to increase numbers of machines and promote innovation in business. This would boost the returns on invested money and cause the general living standards to increase.

Free market economy needed a strong currency to work well. Smith wanted a national currency backed up by precious metals so that the country could not depreciate the nation's money through waste and wars. Starting with this limit on spending, Adam Smith continued with free market government recommendations. They were to maintain low taxes and repeal tariffs so that free trade could flourish over international borders. Smith demonstrated that these tariffs were only hurting the lives of ordinary citizens by raising prices and cutting off trade and industry's efforts overseas.

Limited government proved to be the third big idea that Smith promoted in The Wealth of Nations. Governments should be limited to providing universal education to its citizens, national defense, infrastructure works, and the enforcement of law and justice. Governments were to intervene whenever people pursued short term interests or committed crimes. Larger governments only took money from their ordinary citizens' pockets.

Annual Percentage Rate (APR)

The annual percentage rate, or APR, is the actual interest rate that a loan charges each year. This single percentage number is truthfully used to represent the literal annual expense of using money over the life span of a given loan. Annual percentage rate not only covers interest charged, but can also be comprised of extra costs or fees that are attached to a given loan transaction.

Credit cards and loans commonly offer differing explanations for transaction fees, the structure of their interest rates, and any late fees that are assessed. The annual percentage rate provides an easy to understand formula for expressing to borrowers the real and actual percentage number of fees and interest so that they can measure these up against the rates that other possible lenders will charge them.

Annual percentage rate can include many different elements besides interest. With a nominal APR, it simply involves the rate of a given payment period multiplied out to the exact numbers of payment periods existing in a year. The effective APR is often referred to as the mathematically true rate of interest for a given year. Effective APR’s are commonly the fees charged plus the rate of compound interest.

On a home mortgage, effective annual percentage rates could factor in Private Mortgage Insurance, discount points, and even processing costs. Some hidden fees do not make their ways into an effective APR number. Because of this, you should always read the fine print surrounding an APR and the costs associated with a mortgage or loan. As an example of how an effective APR can be deceptive with mortgages, the one time fees that are charged in the front of a mortgage are commonly assumed to be divided over a loan’s long repayment period. If you only utilize the loan for a short time frame, then the APR number will be thrown off by this. An effective APR on a mortgage might look lower than it actually is when the loan will be paid off significantly earlier than the term of the loan.

The government created the concept of annual percentage rate to stop loan companies and credit cards issuers from deceiving consumers with fancy expressions of interest charges and fees. The law requires that all loan issuers and credit card companies have to demonstrate this annual percentage rate to all customers. This is so the consumers will obtain a fair comprehension of the true rates that are associated with their particular transactions. While credit card companies are in fact permitted to promote their monthly basis of interest rates, they still have to clearly show the actual annual percentage rate to their customers in advance of a contract or agreement being signed by the consumer.

Annual percentage rate is sometimes confused with annual percentage yield. This can be vastly different from the APR. Annual percentage yield includes calculations of compounded interest in its numbers.

Austrian Economics

Austrian Economics arose as a challenge to the then-dominant British tradition of economics originally championed by Adam Smith in his influential across the centuries work *The Wealth of Nations*. It was Carl Menger and his *Principles of Economics* published in 1871 that presented the first alternative to the Imperial British ideas on the workings of the free market system. Menger founded the Austrian School officially, though other had come before him with ideas upon which he built.

Menger was assisted by contemporaries Stanley Jevons and Leon Walras. The trio in their various separate works fleshed out the original ideas of the subjective nature of economic value. It was they who for the first time explained the theories on marginal utility. This was the idea that stated the more units of any good an individual has, the less value he will place on any single unit of them. Menger and company also demonstrated the ways that money begins its life cycle in a free market. The most desirable commodity is wanted not because it can be directly literally consumed, but because it is useful in procuring other goods.

Menger's next influential work was his highly regarded Investigations. This twelve year later published book took on directly the German Historical School that viewed economics as the accruing of data for the benefit of the state. While serving as economics professor at University of Vienna, Menger returned economics back to its roots as the human action based science using deductive logic. He laid the groundwork for the later Austrian Economics' proponents and had students such as Friederich von Wieser who later impacted the critically important Austrian School economist Friedrich von Hayek. Even today, Menger's key works are studied as a fantastic beginning to the economics theory and thinking. All Austrian economists since Menger have considered themselves to be disciples of the great economics school and theory founder Menger.

The next great mind in the Austrian school was follower and admirer of Menger, Eugen Böhm-Bawerk of the University of Innsbruck, Austria. He expanded upon Menger's vast work and repackaged it so that he might apply it to a whole different range of economic questions and challenging topics such as price, value, interest, and capital. His influential work *History and Critique of Interest Theories* was published in 1884 and remains a well-regarded review of the fallacies in the history of philosophy and economics. He first argued that interest rates are an integral component of the market itself. In his later *Positive Theory of Capital*, Böhm-Bawerk proved that the interest rate is actually the normal rate of profit in business.

As a result of these and other works, the Austrian economist battled extensively with the Marxists regarding the ideas of exploitation of capital, refuting the socialist ideas on wages and capital far in advance of the communists arising in Russia. In the final years of Hapsburg Austria, he served three terms as finance minister. This is where he was able to put into place his wise economics theories on sound money and the gold standard, balanced budgets, free trade, and the reversal of monopolies and subsidies for exporters of key goods. His writings, research, and practical application of economics helped to champion the Austrian School all across the Anglo-American and Imperial British world.

A last key Austrian Economics' founding scholar proved to be Ludwig von Mises. He published his perennial *The Theory of Money and Credit*, once again breaking fresh ground for the Austrian School. Here he fleshed out the application of the theory of marginal utility to money. Mises also worked out a full-scale outline of the Austrian School on the business cycle. After the First World War ended, Mises attacked the rising forces of political and economic socialist in his expository series of essays he purloined into the book Socialism. Here he demonstrated effectively how the practical application of socialism to nation states and governments would lead to the complete break down of society and eventually the end of the civilized world. This debate raged on, mostly in favor of the socialists, all the way until the crash of political and economic socialism around the world in 1989. From beyond the grave, von Mises had the last laugh.

Mises was such an influential Austrian Economics thinker that his converts and disciples from the socialist side included legendary Hayek, Lionel Robbins, and Wilhelm Röpke. They went on to lay the ground work for the revival of Austrian Economics in the U.S. and Great Britain still ongoing in the present days. Among his last and most influential of students, Rothbard proved to be one of the most adept proponents of Mises' ideas. He wrote *Man, Economy, and State* in 1963. The revival this began in the then-struggling Austrian School still continues to this day.

Barter

Barter is a concept that pre-dates the invention of money. It proves to be the practice of trading goods, products, or services for other such products, services, and goods. Barter is a simpler way of transacting business, commonly without using money.

Although money systems have been in existence and well established for several thousand years, bartering for things as a practice is still alive and well nowadays. Systems of barter are used much of the time between one nation and another. Countries and companies occasionally engage in the practice as well. Barter is frequent in between businesses, and is sometimes also seen between a person and a business, or two different people. Within the U.S., bartering involves billions of dollars of services and goods that are exchanged back and forth in a single year. Per the International Reciprocal Trade Association that monitors bartering, over 400,000 businesses around the world bartered for more than $11 billion in just 2009.

Barter is sometimes referred to as counter-trade, in particular when it is used between two different countries. Bartering can be supremely convenient for countries that have an abundance of one or more resources or commodities but little cash on hand. Countries that produce huge quantities of wheat might exchange it directly with other countries for produce, oil, or textiles.

Where businesses are concerned, barter usually involves trading out services or products in consideration for advertising. Radio stations, television stations, and newspapers are common participants in barter, who may accept promotional goods for ads or on the air time. Other companies will exchange goods and services for stock in a company, or advice in consideration for services and goods.

Companies and individuals sometimes engage in barter as well. One company might give a consumer free merchandise in exchange for helpful sales leads. Individuals barter between each other for almost any item imaginable. Auction sites represent outlets for trading and bartering things. Interpersonal bartering is also carried out using online and print versions of classified ads. Today there are even barter clubs that help individuals learn more about and practice bartering.

In some countries like Spain, barter markets have arisen and spread. These swap meets forbid the use of money in any transactions. Participants simply bring along unwanted items and trade them with one or more parties for other items that they desire.

In times of national crises, bartering becomes more popular and commonplace. When currencies become victims of hyperinflation or devaluation, barter is resurrected. In these times and situations, barter can even supersede money as the principal medium of exchange.

Benchmarking

Benchmarking is a practice favored across many different industries and individual corporations. It refers to the idea of making a comparison between one's own company, processes, and operations against competing businesses within the entire market or only the businesses' own sector of the market. Companies can carry out this activity utilizing processes, products, approaches, or functions. There are a range of comparison points in such initiatives. Some of the most common include measuring quality, time, customer satisfaction, and effectiveness versus cost.

The goal and idea behind this Benchmarking lies in comparing and contrasting a company's own internal operations as measured against the competitors' own. It aims to create suggestions for bettering approaches, processes, and technologies in order to lower business costs, build up customer satisfaction and brand loyalty, and boost revenues and profits. This Benchmarking proves to be a critical component of initiatives for constantly boosting quality, as with Six Sigma.

There are many reasons that drive companies to benchmark. They often start with the idea that one of their approaches to business or internal processes may be improved somehow. Other corporations will draw these comparisons with competitors in an effort to discover problems within their own internal product delivery or service quality so that they can obtain a competitive advantage. The ultimate motivation in doing this activity lies in measuring up a company against the market leader or best in class corporation in a given industry. Many times companies will benchmark against corporations that are outstanding examples in a different industry to attempt to copy their success at a particular product, process, or method.

It is always helpful to look at a tangible example of a real world case study to better understand the concept. Southwest Airlines today is an industry-leading airline that did not always boast such a stellar reputation. A number of years ago, they notoriously analyzed the approaches, processes, and speed of delivery from pit crews in car racing. They did this with the goal of obtaining actionable ideas on boosting the time of their turn around on the ground and at the gate. As a result of this famous experiment with benchmarking, Southwest Airlines was successful in revamping their gate cleaning, maintenance, and customer boarding operations which helped the company to save one millions of dollars' worth of expenses each year.

Corporations which wish to engage in a benchmarking exercise do not have to come up with all of the data on their own. In fact a number of consumer organizations and industries themselves publish their own comparative data studies which companies can utilize to do a benchmark initiative. As an example, in the industry of used and new cars, Consumer Reports publishes an incredibly detailed section on the test results of both used and new cars. The fact that companies can often purchase such data means that they can pursue such initiatives without having to spend inordinate amounts of time and effort coming up with the comparison data in the first place.

Companies which are keen to boost their own customer service efforts could choose to compare their personal internal processes and measurements versus the ones which the industry leading success story company boasts. When they determine what their shortcomings are in the metrics, they can then decide to strengthen their processes and overall performance. To do this, the benchmarking corporation will study, consider, and then measure the operations of their successful competitor. They might go so far as to dispatch some of their employees to act as customers of the rival in order to obtain real-world experience in what the other company is doing so exceptionally well.

This means that a fast food restaurant chain which needs fast and accurate drive thru service to be successful would consider the efforts and results of its critical competitors. This is not an arbitrary example as the industry companies are well known for continuously studying and benchmarking against the various other competing companies in the sector. The best example of this is Pal's Sudden Service. They have won such prestigious awards for their speed and service that they opened an educational institute that now trains the employers and management of other businesses. A number of fast food corporations consider them to be the world class benchmark for themselves and their own operations.

Boom

A boom is an economic expansion that happens when the economy of a country is growing at a rapid economic pace. Booms are more precisely commonly defined as periods in which the Gross Domestic Product expands at a faster rate pace than the long term economic growth trend rate.

Total demand of goods and merchandise proves to be high in boom periods. Businesses generally respond to this rising demand by boosting production and accompanying employment. Sometimes they will choose to increase their profit margins through raising their prices. Higher demands finally pressure limited resources. If sufficient extra capacity is not present to address the demand, then demand pull inflation can result.

Economic booms are characterized by numerous factors. Increasing, strong demands are mostly pushed by consumption in households. Ultimately, demand is furthermore boosted by exports, fixed investments, and government spending. Export growth results along with an expansion of world trade growth.

Along with greater demand comes higher wages and employment rates. Booms lead to increasingly tighter employment markets and better incomes for those working. This tightness in labor market conditions is most evident in lower unemployment rates. It is also seen in the labor force percentage that is working, the quantities of job openings that are not filled, and reports on labor shortfalls in particular careers and fields. The actual incomes of those people working in boom times increase rapidly as the demand for labor is high and numerous chances exist to increase earnings from higher productivity and more overtime shifts.

In booms, the tax revenues accruing to government rise rapidly as well. This results from rising employment and income levels. This has been called a fiscal dividend that comes from a sustained expansion. A budget surplus typically results that can be utilized to further public spending or to reduce the amount of outstanding government debt.

Booms further see the rising of company investments and profits. These in turn often result in greater amounts of capital investments. The amount and strength of the given demand has a great impact on how many investments are planned during the boom.

Productivity also rises during booms. These booms that happen in cycles are healthy for the productivity of labor. This is because in these times, businesses stretch their employees and resources to keep up with the additional demand by utilizing the companies' resources more effectively and intensely. Productivity rises as a direct result.

Booms commonly also increase a country's demand for goods and services that are imported. This is especially the case in countries that are huge importers in general, such as the United States and Great Britain. Rising imports lead to higher trade deficits, which have to be offset with cash or debt in payment.

Brexit

Brexit refers to the Jun 23, 2016 referendum on the future of Britain in the European Union. The term comes from the Grexit reference to the potential for Greece to leave the Eurozone shared currency area in past years. In this historic referendum, British voters have to answer the question “Should the UK remain a member of the EU or leave the EU?” Britain’s electoral commission came up with the phrasing of the question and parliament accepted it.

The question of having a referendum on the issue arose in the 2015 general election in the U.K. Prime Minister David Cameron promised voters that he would offer the British people a final say on the issue of remaining in the EU if he won reelection. His ruling conservative party has been split on the Euro-skeptic idea and EU membership for around 40 years. The individual on the ground Conservative members are largely for exiting from the European Union over a variety of issues of sovereignty and border and legal control.

Those in favor of Britain leaving the EU believe that the restrictive rules hamper creation of new jobs. They also want to be able to decide on which laws to pass and on their trading partners. Though parliament in London passes laws, these can and have been overturned by the European Parliament and courts in Brussels.

Part of the reason the government decided to hold the referendum in early summer was to have it over before the next summer migration crisis begins in earnest. This migration problem has recently stirred up anger and fear in British citizens that they are losing control of their migration policy to the European Union in Brussels. Proponents of the leave campaign want to make their own immigration policy and decide on who comes into the country.

Those in favor of staying in the EU have their own reasons for their position. They feel that remaining in the block of European countries increases the nation’s economic, military, and global influence around the world. Remain campaigners argue that Britain is stronger and more secure at home and abroad by being a part of this largest economic block in the world.

The voting base for this historic referendum is different than for general elections. Any British citizen who is older than 18 is allowed to vote. Citizens of the Commonwealth of Nations who reside in Britain are also eligible to cast ballots. There are 53 member nations of the Commonwealth. This means that residents in Britain of such countries and entities as Canada, Australia, New Zealand, Ireland, Malta, Cyprus, and Gibraltar will be allowed to vote on the Brexit issue.

Brexit supports have argued that the European Union has many incentives to continue trading with the United Kingdom. It remains a large importer of services and goods and carries out much of its trade with the block. They feel that they will be able to forge new and better trade agreements with the rest of the world. This would save them more than 8 billion pounds in contributions made to the European Union budget every year. They believe that the country will be able to join Norway, Iceland, and Liechtenstein as a European Economic Area member nation.

Those who favor remaining in the EU argue that leaving the block will create too much uncertainty in British markets. They argue that foreign companies will not be so likely to invest in Britain and others may move their EU regional or international headquarters to other countries should Britain cease to have unfettered access to the common market.

The Treasury has predicted that a recession created by leaving the EU block would cost households 4,300 Pounds per year in lost jobs, trade, and higher taxes by the year 2030. They argue that the pound will weaken substantially and push up the costs for weekly shopping, travel, and imported goods. Others are worried about what will happen to outside Europeans living in Britain and British expatriates who live around Europe after an exit from the European Union.

Bull Market

A bull market is one in which an entire financial market or a select grouping of securities sees rising prices over an extended period of time. It is also used to describe a scenario in which prices are expected to rise. While the phrase bull market is most frequently utilized to address the stock markets, it can similarly reference any items that trade, such as sustained rising prices in commodities, currencies, or bonds. The opposite of a bull market is a bear market.

The simplest definition of a bull market is one that is rising. Bull markets are those that witness an increase in prices of market shares that is sustained for a period of time. In bull markets, investors show great confidence that this rising trend will only continue to exist over a longer term. When bull markets are in effect, a nation's economy remains strong and employment levels prove to be higher.

Bull markets show the characteristics of high investor confidence, general enthusiasm about the future, and anticipation that strong and successful results will continue to occur. Forecasting with any certainty when such bull market trends will wane is challenging. Much of the problem lies in attempting to decipher speculation's role and the psychological impacts of investors that can often have a major influence on the markets in general.

Bull markets in stocks commonly develop as an economic slow down is waning. They begin in advance of an economy demonstrating a convincing recovery. As investors' confidence levels grow, they show this by their buying and investing in a belief that stock prices will gain in the future. Bull markets generally turn out to be positive and winning scenarios for most investors.

The phrase bull market is derived from the animal world, as is its opposite concept of bear markets. Bulls attack their prey by using their horns in an upward thrust, as when markets are moving up. Bears on the other hand swipe their victims down with their paws, as when markets are falling down. When the trend is rising, the market is a bull market. When it is falling instead, it is called a bear market.

Examples of bull markets abound in both the United States and developing countries. Throughout most of the 1980’s and 1990’s, the U.S. stock markets rose in a long running bull market. Prices rose by nearly ten fold in that time period. The Dot Com bubble put an end to this bull market at the turn of the century.

Around the world, there have also been numerous bull markets in foreign stock exchanges. In India, the Bombay Stock Exchange, known as SENSEX, experienced a dramatic bull market for five years from mid 2003 to the first of 2008. In this time frame, the index ran from 2,900 points on up to 21,000 points.

Bureau of Economic Analysis (BEA)

The Bureau of Economic Analysis is also known by its acronym the BEA. It is a bureau within the United States Department of Commerce. This BEA develops and publishes statistics for economic accounts that help a variety of groups to make decisions and to understand the economic performance of the U.S. Among the parties that follow their publications and statistics are business and government leaders, researchers, and members of the American public.

The publications which the Bureau of Economic Analysis produces prove to be among the most critical statistics of economics in the country. This includes such national benchmark economic indicators as the GDP Gross Domestic Product along with the balance of payments. The PCE Personal Consumption Expenditures Index is also compiled and released as part of their national economic data.

These and other statistics which the Bureau of Economic Analysis publishes have significant impact on important decisions in the U.S. Public policymakers, consumer households, individual people, and business heads use these numbers. They impact such important business, personal, and economic fundamentals as exchange rates, interest rates, budget and tax forecasts, investment plans for businesses, and the distribution of federal funds. These federal government grant monies total in excess of $390 billion. Numerous agencies distribute them to local and state organizations and communities.

Besides the two national bell weather statistics of GDP and balance of payments, the Bureau of Economic Analysis also puts together and publishes a variety of regional, national, international, and industry specific economic accounts. These deliver crucial information on a range of issues. Among these are relationships between various industries, economic development on a regional basis, and the position of the United States in the global economy as a whole.

Chief among the important statistics the Bureau of Economic Analysis keeps and uses are the NIPAs National Income and Product Accounts. They serve as a cornerstone for all of the agencies' other national and regional statistics. They include the country's gross domestic product numbers and other relevant measurements.

Many individuals are not aware of the depth of the international statistics which the Bureau of Economic Analysis keeps and provides on its website. Their international trade and investment country facts cover all of the nations in the world. These statistics are essentially complete reports on each nation's trade and direct foreign investment with the United States.

They provide information on the exports from and imports to the U.S. from each country. They also showcase the dollar amount of direct foreign investment to and from America for each nation selected. Included in this information is a detailed breakdown of the different types of imports, exports, and trade goods exchanged between each country selected and the United States.

Regional reports which the BEA provides cover GDP on a state by state and metropolitan area basis. They also deliver information on each state's and local area personal income throughout the country. The PCE Personal Consumption Expenditures is provided on a state wide level under this category of information as well.

For industry reports, the BEA offers a GDP by industry report and statistics. They also offer an annual industry accounts section which includes a 50 year survey of current business input-output and GDP figures.

Bureau of Engraving and Printing (BEP)

The Bureau of Engraving and Printing is the Treasury Department entity that actually makes the United States' currency. Their mission centers on creating and producing American currency notes which are trusted around the world. They have a vision to be considered the world standard for securities printing. This is so that they can deliver the public and their customers with the best products that are exceptionally well designed and manufactured.

The main activities of the BEP are to print up billions of Federal Reserve notes (or dollars) every single year. They then deliver these to the Federal Reserve System for distribution into the economy. It is the Federal Reserve that exists to be the American central bank. They bear the responsibility to be certain that sufficient coins and bills currency are in active circulation. The BEP handles all of the U.S. printed bills but does not make any coins. United States coins are always minted at the U.S. Mint.

When various federal agencies have concerns or questions about document security, they turn to the BEP for help and advice. The BEP also engages in research and development for improving their utilization of automation processes in production. They are always seeking out technologies to deter counterfeiters of U.S. currency and security documents as well.

It is no understatement to say that currency creation at the BEP offices has changed drastically from its origins in 1862. In those early years, they used the basement in the Treasury building. Here a handful of individuals worked with hand cranked machines to print and separate notes. Today's BEP does not engage in an easy process or job.

Nowadays making the currency bills takes greatly skilled and expertly trained craftspeople who work with specially designed equipment. They utilize both sophisticated and world leading technology alongside the time tested old world printing methods. Producing the currency takes numerous specific steps. This starts with designing, engraving, and making the plates. The specially sourced paper is then plate printed and inspected. Bills are numbered and re-inspected again before being packaged and shipped to their customer the Federal Reserve Bank.

The Bureau of Engraving and Printing also offers redemption of mutilated currency services and the sale of shredded currency. BEP will redeem such mutilated currency for free for the public. If the bills are so damaged that the value can not be conclusively determined, they can be sent on to the BEP so that their trained experts can examine them. After their determination is made, they will redeem the currency for full face value.

They accept currency that has been mutilated by water, fire, chemicals, or explosives; deterioration or petrification from burying; or insect, animal, or rodent damage. Bills missing security features are also treated as mutilated. For them to consider these bills without supporting documentation and explanations for what happened, at least half of the note has to be identifiable as American currency and remain.

If less than 50% is present, Treasury will require proof that the rest of the currency has been destroyed. Each year the department examines 30,000 mutilated currency claims and redeems them for more than $30 million.

The BEP also sells bags of shredded currency as novelty souvenir items. The Fort Worth and Washington, D.C. BEP visitor centers offer them in pre-packed small amounts for those who just want to have some. The D.C. visitor center and online store of the BEP also sell larger five pound bags of such shredded currency. In order to obtain larger quantities, individuals must get permission from the Treasury department and obtain them from one of the Federal Reserve Banks.

Case Shiller Index

The Case Shiller Index represents the collection of United States' Home Price Indices. These were developed by economists Karl Case and noted Yale Professor Robert Shiller. The two men's company Case Shiller Weiss, Inc. produced the statistics from 1991-2002. Allan Weiss their partner oversaw the production and release of the index on a regular basis.

This index is a collection of house price indicators for where the market has come and currently is. Among the many versions of the Case Shiller Index is the 20 city composite, the 10 city composite, and also twenty metro individual regions. The commercial versions of the Case Shiller Indices data points start in January of 1987 and run to date.

CoreLogic has since taken over the production of the index where David Stiff and Linda Ladner assumed direction. There is now a wide variety in this Case Shiller Index because Standard & Poor's 500 produces and owns a number of them. For example, Standard & Poor's publishes the Case Shiller twenty cities, condominium indices, high, medium, and low tier home price indices, and the national U.S. index. Anyone who is interested in following them can do so on the S&P company website. Eleven of the various S&P produced indices can be traded as futures on the Chicago Mercantile Exchange. Standard and Poor's set their value to a level of 100 for the prices based in January 2000.

Robert Shiller and Karl Case calculated the original Case Shiller Index on a different basis. Their index gathered home price data back to 1890. In their calculations, the 100 value was based on the house prices for the index in 1890. Robert Shiller's version of the index on his website comes out quarterly. His calculations are probably different than the ones Standard and Poor's uses as is his reference point. This is why in 2013 for the fourth quarter, the S&P 20 city index showed in the 160s, while the same point for Robert Shiller's data was in the 130s.

Professor Shiller wrote and published a book in 2000 about the housing market called Irrational Exuberance. In this book, he made the statement that no other country in the world seems to have published this type of housing data going back to the 1890s.

There are some important economic inferences that the Case Shiller Index shows. Shiller also detailed these in his book. He insists the idea that housing prices have been in a continuing uptrend over time in the United States is false. Instead, the prices of houses have a powerful tendency to go back towards their levels in 1890 as adjusted for inflation. He also notes that there is no correlation between changing home price patterns and the changes in population levels, interest rates, or even construction costs.

The Case Shiller Index also gives Shiller enough information to explain why there is no constant uptrend in the inflation adjusted home prices. Part of this is mobility. He has stated that if the prices of houses rise enough then people can simply move to another area of the country. This is because urban land makes up less than 3% of the U.S. total land area.

Improvements in technology are another reason Shiller has discussed for this phenomenon. As technology of home construction has consistently improved, it has become quicker and less expensive to build houses. This keeps a lid on the inflation adjusted cost of homes.

Between these reasons, Shiller argues that there is no trend in home prices either up or down. He has observed this not only in the United States, but also in other countries. The real house price indices of Norway and the Netherlands show the same truth.

Central Bank

Central banks are national monetary authorities or reserve banks that are given the unique privilege and responsibility of loaning a government its currency. Central banks have many of the same characteristics that traditional banks do, such as charging set rates of interest on loans that they make to borrowers like the government of the country that they represent, or alternatively to commercial banks in dire need and as a last resort.

Central banks are different from regular banks in a variety of interest ways. Chief among these is their monopoly of creating the nation's currency. They also have the power to loan such currency out to their government as fully legal tender. These banks are the only ones that will lend to commercial banks in difficult times of need, too.

The main role of a central bank is to issue and oversee a country's supply of money. Besides this, they also engage in a number of more vigorous activities including setting and monitoring the interest rates of subsidized loans and helping out the banking sector in periods of financial difficulties or even crisis. Some central banks additionally supervise the commercial banking sector and individual banks in order to make certain that they do not engage in corrupt behavior or rash decision making and practices.

Not all countries possess central banks that are independent of the other branches of government's meddling and interference. Most of the wealthy countries of the world do have this type of central bank in a system that stops politicians from intervening in monetary policy. The European Central Bank, Bank of England, and Federal Reserve System of the United States are all good examples of independent central banks. Central banks can be privately held or publicly owned. In the U.S., the Federal Reserve proves to be a unique combination of private and public components.

Central banks are involved in many important functions. These include carrying out monetary policy and fixing the nation's interest rates. They also control their country's whole money supply. They act as both banker for the government and for all of a country's banks in difficult times. Central banks similarly handle the nation's gold reserves and foreign exchange reserves.

They may adjust these by buying or selling more gold, or by balancing the amount and kinds of currencies that they hold at any time. Many central banks supervise their banking industries as well, though not all perform this function. Central banks also help to deal with and combat inflation and manage a country's currency exchange rate by modifying the nation's official interest rates and utilizing similar policies to ensure that the desired outcomes of low inflation and stable currency exchange rates are in fact achieved.

Closeout Sale

A closeout sale represents the last sale for a given item from a retailer. It could also refer to the last offers from a retailer in its inventory it provides to the public or another company. Sometimes certain items simply are not selling effectively. Other time it may be that a retailer is forced to sell off its inventory thanks to a fire, moving to another location, or too much inventory. In many cases, the company has simply gone bankrupt and has to liquidate everything. In these last cases, this type of sale is also referred to as a “going out of business sale.”

Car dealerships also offer these types of inventory-moving events following hail storms. These are called “hail sales” in this case because the car dealership inventory has suffered extensive damage from the inclement weather. In any of these last chance scenarios, stores or outlets make an effort to get the word out to their customers and the general buying public.

A closeout sale should never be confused with a closeout store. These outlets are stores that concentrate their efforts on purchasing wholesale closeout items off of retailers. They then sell them to their own customer base for a price discount. In the United States, there are several nationally known examples of this type of operation. Closeout store chains include Big Lots, Marshalls, Ross Dress for Less, TJ Maxx, and Value City. They mostly specialize in goods that are house ware or clothes related.

It is a well-known fact that many times, items purchased in closeout sale offers cannot be returned according to the company policy of many stores. The goal is to move these items, not exchange them for other closeout sale items. In the cases of store closing and liquidation efforts, this is usually the policy. In other jurisdictions outside of the United States, like the United Kingdom, the buying customers maintain their typical rights of return in any sale. This means that they are allowed to return defective goods under the country’s Distance Selling Regulations.

Holiday-themed merchandise is often the subject of closeout sales in the U.S. and other Western nation economies. This is because it is expensive and space-intensive to store Christmas merchandise for the better part of a year. Most American stores therefore engage in after-Christmas clearance sales. Some of them even commence ahead of the holidays. The discounts at such events can typically be 25 percent or more, though they actually range from five percent to as high as 50 percent. Sometimes stores will later boost this discount from 75 percent to even 90 percent rather than store the final merchandise, allowing it to age. In Canada, these post-Christmas sales are called “Boxing Day sales.” They attract enormous shopping crowds looking for their closeout deals following Christmas.

Merchandise which is specific to a given season is often seen at clearance sales. This is especially true for winter wear or summer time patio furniture. This allows the store to bring out more current styles and fashions in their limited showroom or shelf space.

Thrift stores that are normally better priced than traditional big box department stores also practice what they call “rolling” closeouts. In these stores, they simply take all of the merchandise which they offer in a particular week and tag it with a special color or sometimes letter to make it clear which items are part of the closeout sale. In these cases, they rotate out the clearance goods once per month.

In the more traditional department stores, they also utilize closeout sales in their physical locations. They will take merchandise they wish to discontinue and place it on their clearance racks. The price will continue to drop until the point that a shopper finally takes the item to buy it. Stores have taken this concept and reproduced it on online in recent years. The first Internet-based operation to imitate the retail store clearance idea was the now-failed Drop.com. They permitted sellers on the site to auto reduce the price of their items for the online customers.

Collaboration

Collaboration proves to be a process where two or more individuals or entities choose to work in concert on behalf of a common goal or endeavor. Intellectual enterprises and other activities that tend to be creative by their nature are often most effectively accomplished through collaboration, which involves learning together, mutually sharing knowledge, and building up consensus. Scientific collaboration is very common because of this.

Most forms of collaboration must have leadership. Such leadership does not have to be in the form of traditional command structures, but can instead be social leadership affected in a group of equals or alternatively that is decentralized. Reasons for practicing collaboration are fairly evident. Teams working together in collaboration have access to a greater number of resources, rewards, and recognition when they compete for limited resources.

Collaboration can be extremely structured. When it is set up like this, then inward looking communication and behavior are encouraged. Such forms of collaboration particularly attempt to boost teams' successes as they work on problem solving in collaboration. Charts, graphs, rubrics, and forms are all utilized in this type of collaboration in order to lay out personalities and personal characteristics without bias, so that the future and present projects' collaboration will be bettered.

In business and finance, collaboration can be as simple as a partnership or as complicated as a multinational corporation. Team members that work together in an organization using collaboration achieve superior communication both in the business supply chains and the entire outfit. Such collaboration proves to be a means of putting together the various ideas and concepts of a wide variety of individuals in order to assemble a great range of knowledge and information. This proves to be invaluable to businesses and other organizations that require both general and specialist forms of knowledge from as many viable sources as possible.

Mass collaboration has become a reality as a result of fairly recent technological innovations. These include wireless Internet, high speed Internet, and various Internet based tools for collaboration, such as wikis, blogs, and others. Through these means, individuals from literally all over the planet can effectively share ideas and discourse back and forth via the Internet and even Internet based conferences, without being limited to certain geographical locations or challenges. Thanks to these forms of collaboration in both business and other forms, the possibilities of improving a project's results are practically endless.

Commercial Banks

Commercial banks are those financial institutions which offer a wide range of financial services to a variety of clients. Chief among these services are issuing loans and receiving deposits. The customers of such commercial financial institutions are able to avail themselves of a broad range of investment products that such banks offer. Included in these are certificates of deposit and savings accounts. Such banks issue a wide variety of loans which range from car loans and business loans to home equity loans and mortgages.

Banks which are commercial in nature deliver a range of financial products like checking accounts, savings accounts, and certificates of deposit. Customers of banks prefer these kinds of financial products since they are guaranteed by the FDIC Federal Deposit Insurance Corporation within the U.S.

In consideration for their funds' deposit, the commercial banks provide interest to their clients against their deposits. This is how these institutions realize profit--- they utilize the deposits of their customers to make loans that bring in higher interest rates than the ones they offer to their depositors. This spread from the amount the banks are paying out to the ones it is gathering back in becomes the net interest income of the commercial banks.

Such financial institutions do not all offer the same exact loan products to their various customers. They may specialize in several types or only a single kind of loan. These commercial banks are able to provide mortgages to purchase homes and home equity loans. In these cases, the houses provide the collateral to underlie the loans. Such financial institutions also provide auto loans with the vehicles as the loan collateral. The institutions similarly deliver personal loans, credit cards, and lines of credit to well-qualified borrowers.

Besides the interest such banks earn for their loans on the books, they can also create income through levying fees on their customers for banking services. This is common on products including checking and savings accounts, credit cards, and especially mortgage applications and originations.

There has been an evolution within the universe of commercial banks over the last two decades. Institutions that originally began as traditionally physical "brick and mortar" outlets complete with bank tellers, ATM's, bank vaults, and safe deposit boxes are still dominant. Yet a new and powerful challenger has arisen. This is the story of the commercial bank without physical branch locations.

Such virtual banks, or online only banks, lack physical branches. They force customers to do all of their transactions either over the Internet or by phone banking. The trade off for this accommodation is that these financial institutions deliver higher interest rates for accounts, deposits, and investments as their overheads are substantially lower. They also tend to charge significantly smaller and fewer fees. They can do this since they lack all of the associated costs which come with property taxes, rents, utilities, and additional staff salaries and benefits.

It is important to realize that the activities of commercial banking are vastly different than those of their colleagues in investment banking. With investment banking, the institutions engage in a number of stock and financial markets-related businesses. Among these are financial markets underwriting, performing tasks as intermediaries between the investors of and issuers of securities, fostering and participating in mergers and acquisitions and various kinds of corporate restructurings, and performing services as primary broker on behalf of institutional clients.

Other commercial banks boast investment banking divisions. This means that they are both involved in commercial banking and investment banking all at once. These include such well-known and enormous American financial institutions as JPMorgan Chase and Citibank and the multinational giant British banks like HSBC and Barclays. Other operations including Ally focus exclusively on the commercial banking segment of the industry.

Commodities

Commodities turn out to be items that are taken from the earth, such as orange juice, cattle, wheat, oil, and gold. Companies buy commodities to turn them into usable products like bread, gasoline, and jewelry to sell to other businesses and consumers. Individual investors purchase and sell them for the purposes of speculation, in an attempt to make a profit.

Commodities are traded through commodities brokers on one of several different commodities exchanges, such as COMEX, or the Commodities Mercantile Exchange, NYMEX, or the New York Mercantile Exchange, and NYBOT, or the New York Board of Trade, among others.

Commodities are traded with contracts using a great amount of leverage. This means that with a small amount of money, a great quantity of the commodity in question can be controlled and traded. For example, with only a few thousand dollars, you as an investor are able to control a contract of one thousand barrels of heating oil or one hundred ounces of gold.

As a result of this high leverage that you obtain, the amounts of money made or lost can be significant with only relatively small moves in the price of the underlying commodity. This leverage results from the fact that commodities are nearly always traded using margin accounts that lead to significant risks for the capital invested. For example, with gold contracts, each ten cent minimum price move represents a $10 per contract gain or loss.

Commodity trading strategies center around speculation on factors that will affect the production of a commodity. These could be related to weather, natural disasters, strikes, or other events. If you believed that severe hurricanes would damage a great portion of the Latin American coffee crop, then you would call your commodity broker and instruct them to buy as many coffee contracts as they had money in the account to cover.

If the hurricanes took place and coffee did see significant damage in the region, then the prices of coffee would rise dramatically as a result of the negative weather, causing the coffee harvest to be more valuable. Your coffee contracts would similarly rise in value, probably significantly.

A variety of commodities can be traded on the commodities exchanges. These include grains, metals, energy, livestock, and softs. Grains consistently prove to be among the most popular of commodities available to trade. Grain commodities are usually most active in the spring and summer. Grains include soybeans, corn, oats, wheat, and rough rice.

Metals commodities offer you the opportunity to take positions on precious metals such as gold and silver. Changes in the underlying prices of base metals may also be traded in this category. Metals include copper, silver, and gold.

Energy commodities that you can trade are those used for heating homes and fueling vehicles for the nation. With the energy complex you can trade on supply disruptions around the world or higher gas prices that you anticipate. Energy commodities available to you are crude oil, unleaded gas, heating oil, and natural gas.

Livestock includes animals that provide pork and beef. Because these are staple foods in most American diets, they provide among the more reliable pattern trends for trading. Pork bellies, lean hogs, and live cattle are all examples of tradable livestock commodities.

Softs are comprised of both food and fiber types of commodities. Many of these are deemed to be exotic since they are grown in other countries and parts of the earth. Among the soft markets that you can trade are sugar, coffee, cocoa, cotton, orange juice, and lumber.

Commodity Money

There are several forms of money which have been used throughout history. The oldest and best proven form is known as commodity money. A form of money invented in the past century which has become the major competitor to this historical currency is called fiat money. A newer post-modern technologically advanced form of spending power is today's electronic money. All three have their pros and cons, yet the arguments about commodities being safe and trusted keep them alive despite their critics colorfully referring to them as barbaric relics of ancient history.

Commodity money is that type of money that possesses intrinsic value on its own, independent of any governing body. This means the money itself contains its own worth. It is not merely a token or representative of financial value as with bank notes or numbers on a computer screen and in a ledger. The longest reigning and best loved form of commodity money remains gold and silver coins. Their history is legendary and stretches back five thousand years through times good, bad, and tragic.

Any type of commodity is able to fulfill the role of commodity money. As long as the money's value springs from the material from which it is comprised and not some arbitrary decree of a ruler or government representative, it is in fact hard money. Numerous commodities in various times and places have been effectively utilized as this form of tired and true currency. Besides gold and silver, peoples, nations, and empires have employed salt, chocolate beans, copper, decorative belts, shells, cigarettes, and even large stones. Critics have argued that many of these forms of currency were prone to spoilage or gradual deterioration.

The overwhelming majority of cash forms with which people buy and sell nowadays lack any intrinsic value whatsoever. Banknotes are a case in point. They are fiat money. This is money that only contains any value because the government decrees it has the full faith and credit of the nation backing it. It works because members of society and businesses choose to accept it as their primary form of currency and means of exchanging goods and services.

It is interesting that commodity money does not have to be inherently useful to the owner to have value for exchange. Few people have practical uses for gold or silver coins. These coins have dramatically high value because goldsmiths and jewelers are able to utilize them to produce costly jewelry or collectible items of great worth and because of their inherent scarcity.

When societies choose to utilize such commodity money as metal coins for their official legal tender, it is up to the government in question to determine the fixed value of each coin in the currency lineup. The face value of these coins is the one that will be accepted rather than the value of the metal contained within each piece.

Coins are usually circulated at a face value that is greater than the costs of the underlying metal materials. There are some cases, as with runaway inflation, where coins can have greater metal value than face value. This is especially the case with coins made mostly or entirely from gold or silver. When this is a persistent problem, governments often attack the problem by taking that currency unit out of circulation.

Fiat money is the opposite of this commodity money. Fiat money only derives its value from legal claims and obligations of the law. It is truly like a purchase voucher which can be utilized to exchange for services and goods. This means that its purchasing power varies. Fiat money only has fixed value in settling debts. Originally it emerged as a means of convenience so that individuals could carry lighter paper certificates that the government guaranteed rather than having to ship and guard heavy gold and silver.

Over time, governments stealthily stopped exchanging this paper money for the gold and silver that originally backed it. Fiat money is now useless intrinsically and can not be redeemed for any commodity as it once could. The only reason it has any value at all is because the government says it will be valued for that purpose.

Commonwealth of Nations

The Commonwealth of Nations is a voluntary membership organization that counts 52 different equal and independent sovereign countries on its roster. Within these nations live 2.2 billion citizens. More than 60% of these residents are less than 30 years old.

Included in the Commonwealth are countries which are among the smallest and largest as well as poorest and richest in the world. The member nations hail from five different regions including Europe, North America, South America, Africa, and Asia/Oceania. Fully thirty one of the members of this organization are smaller countries, a number of them being island states.

The Commonwealth of Nations' history stretches back to the days of the British Empire. This makes it among the oldest political groups of countries in the entire world. The vast majority of nations in the club were once ruled indirectly or directly by Great Britain. Many of these states chose to become independent and self governing even when they kept the monarch of Britain as their Head of State.

They created the Commonwealth in 1949 as a successor organization to the empire. In the years since then, other nations from the Americas, Africa, Europe, Asia, and the Pacific have also become members. The two most recent nations to join were Mozambique and Rwanda. Neither one had a historical connection to the British Empire.

Leaders of Commonwealth of Nations countries meet together every other year in order to discuss pressing issues of shared concern. Queen Elizabeth has attended all but one of the meetings since the organization began in 1949. The last meeting held in 2016 took place in Malta in the Mediterranean Sea. The next meeting is scheduled to occur in the United Kingdom in 2018.

Today membership in the Commonwealth of Nations is a matter of equal and free cooperation which is voluntary. The nations making up the Commonwealth count on the support of over 80 intergovernmental, professional, cultural, and civil society organizations. They ascribe to a body of guiding principles which are found in the Commonwealth Charter. The group participates in a variety of projects to improve aspects of infrastructure, education, health, and all around society in its member states.

One of the important leadership institutions within the Commonwealth of Nations is the Commonwealth Secretariat. This office leads and guides the group with technical assistance, policy making, and advisory help to member states of the Commonwealth. It works to support governments in their quest to build development that is equitable, inclusive, and sustainable. Its work strives to encourage rule of law, democracy, good government, human rights, and economic and social development. It gives a platform for small countries and helps to empower the youth. The most important work of the organization is laid out at the biannual Commonwealth Head of Government Meetings (CHOGM).

The vision of the Commonwealth of Nations is to work to form and sustain an organization that strives towards mutual peace, prosperity, resilience, and respect while cherishing diversity, equality, and shared values. The Commonwealth's mission is to empower member state governments while it works with the overall Commonwealth nations and other countries in order to better the lives of every Commonwealth citizen and to help move forward their mutual interests around the world.

Consumer Debt

Consumer debt refers to debts which individuals owe because of goods they have purchased. These goods must be consumable forms which do not appreciate in value to qualify for the designation. Having huge amounts of consumer debts is generally considered to be negative for individuals since it raises the burden on their resources to keep up with the debt servicing. It also makes it harder to remit the installment payments which are often laden with interest. When these types of debts are not well managed, they can cause a consumer to be forced into bankruptcy.

There are cases where some analysts and economists feel that a little consumer debt can benefit the individual. These scenarios mostly center on instances where the debt is run up in purchasing an asset that will increase the earning power of the individual. Several examples of this are useful to consider. One of them surrounds buying a car with financing in order to reach a job which pays more. Another might be incurring student debt to obtain a higher degree that will make it possible to secure a promotion or better job.

There are differences between this consumer debt and those that governments or businesses owe. Consumer debt is also referred to as consumer credit. This type of debt can be obtained from credit unions, commercial banks, and sometimes the United States federal government. Among the two categories of consumer debt are revolving debt and non-revolving debt.

Revolving debt is represented by credit cards. These debts are called revolving as they were originally intended to be repaid every month when the bill comes due. In practice this does not often happen, as consumers carry balances forward much of the time. Non-revolving debts are fixed installment payment loans. They are not paid off fully in a typical given month. They are more commonly held against the underlying asset's useful life. Mortgages on homes are not considered to be consumer debt. Rather they are counted as personal forms of investment in real estate under the category of personal residential.

As of January 2017, the total debt of American consumers increased to $3.77 trillion. This represented a 2.8 percent increase over the prior month.

Around $2.78 trillion of this consumer debt was comprised of non-revolving loans. It had grown by 5.5 percent. Debts on credit cards represented $995 billion at this point. This had dropped by 4.6 percent in January versus December of 2016.

There are three reasons why Americans find themselves so deeply in debt today. These are school loans, car loans, and credit cards. School loans commonly last for ten years. They can also be pushed to an over 25 year repayment schedule by extension. The federal government guarantees most of these loans since there are no assets with which to back a college degree. The rates are low to encourage higher education. During the Great Recession, these loan defaults skyrocketed as the loans increased massively with many people who were unemployed "going back to school" to improve their prospects. The Affordable Care Act gave the Federal government authority to take over this national student loan program from Sallie Mae, the private company which previously administered it.

Car loans typically run from three to five years, which is considered to be the safe collateral life of the new vehicle. After this point, the value of these cars depreciates so highly that they are no longer considered to be valuable collateral. Banks simply repossess the vehicle if the borrowers default on the payment schedule. There are more of these loans now thanks to the low interest rates which encourage borrowing to buy vehicles.

Finally, credit card debt soared because of the Bankruptcy Protection Act of 2005. People could no longer easily declare bankruptcy, so they were forced to run up their credit cards in an effort to pay bills, especially healthcare. In July of 2008, the credit card debt peaked at its historic high of $1.028 trillion. This amounted to a per household average of $8,640.

Consumer Price Index (CPI)

The Consumer Price Index, also known by its acronym of CPI, actually measures changes that take place over time in the level of the pricing of various consumer goods and services that American households buy. The Bureau of Labor Statistics in the U.S. says that the Consumer Price Index is a measurement of the over time change in the prices that urban consumers actually pay for a certain grouping of consumer goods and services.

This consumer price index is not literal in the sense of what inflation really turns out to be. Instead, it is a statistical estimate that is built utilizing the costs of a basket of sample items that are supposed to be representative for the entire economy. These goods and services' prices are ascertained from time to time. In actual practice, both sub indices such as clothing, and even sub-sub indices, such as men's dress shirts, are calculated for varying sub-categories of services and goods. These are then taken and added together to create the total index. The different goods are assigned varying weights as shares of the total amount of the expenditures of consumers that the index covers.

Two essential pieces of information are necessary to build the consumer price index. These are the weighting data and the pricing data. Weighting data comes from estimates of differing kinds of expenditure shares as a percentage of the entire expenditure that the index covers. Sample household expenditure surveys are sourced to figure what the weightings should be. Otherwise, the National Income and Product Accounts estimates of expenditures on consumption are utilized. Pricing data is gathered from a sampling of goods and services taken from a sample range of sales outlets in varying locations and at a sampling of times.

The consumer price index is figured up monthly in the United States. Some other countries determine their CPI's on a quarterly basis. The different components of the consumer price index include food, clothing, and housing, all of which are weighted averages of the sub-sub indices. The CPI index literally compares the prices of one month with the prices in the reference month.

Consumer Price Index is only one of a few different pricing indices that the majority of national statistical agencies calculate. Inflation is figured up using the yearly percentage changes in the underlying consume price index. Uses of this CPI can include adjusting real values of pensions, salaries, and wages for inflation's effects, as well as for monitoring costs, and showing alterations in actual values through deflating the monetary magnitudes. The CPI and US National Income and Product Accounts prove to be among the most carefully followed of economic indicators.

Cost of living index is another measurement that is generated based on the consumer price index. It demonstrates how much consumer expenditures need to adjust to compensate for changes in prices. This details how much consumers need to keep up a constant standard of living.

Core CPI

Core CPI refers to the Consumer Price Index. This term revolves around the idea of core inflation. It reveals the longer term price trend in a given item or economy. Core CPI is a means of measuring inflation which leaves out some specific items, particularly those that experience volatility in their pricing. There is a reason for excluding these items. To learn what long term inflation actually is, volatility in prices over the short term and temporary price changes have to be eliminated.

Core inflation is most typically figured up by using the core CPI. This takes out some products like food and energy items, especially oil and gas. Both of these categories may experience short term price changes. Such short term shocks often differ from the bigger picture trend in inflation and provide a false reading of it.

There is another way of calculating core CPI. This is called the outlier method. This way of figuring core inflation takes away products that show the biggest price movements. Many of these items' prices fluctuate rapidly in commodity markets when speculators trade them for profit. Since their prices do not reflect actual alterations of supply and demand, it can make sense to exclude them.

The government is very concerned about which method of measuring inflation it uses. The Federal Reserve decided to switch from CPI to the PCE Index back in January of 2012. They prefer PCE because it offers trends in inflation which are less dramatically impacted by changes in short term prices. Different agencies find other ways to get to what they believe are more accurate means of measuring inflation.

The BEA Bureau of Economic Administration is concerned with eliminating those short term price changes that speculators and traders cause. To get around this, the BEA works with the gross domestic product numbers that already exist and calculates price changes from it. It then takes the monthly release of Retail Survey numbers and measures them against the CPI data-provided consumer prices. The BEA eliminates irregular fluctuations in the inflation data this way and gains more accurate long term trend information.

Determining core CPI inflation is important. It reveals the correlations between goods and services with their prices and the purchasing value of the general income of consumers. Should the costs of goods and services go up in a given time frame while the consumers' parallel income levels do not rise, the buying power of consumers is weakening. This is because their money's actual value is declining when measured against the costs of critical goods and services.

The process could be virtuous as well. Sometimes inflation occurs only on the income of consumers while the costs of goods and services remain constant. In this case, consumers gain greater purchasing power. This means that they will be able to buy an additional amount of the identical services and goods. Asset inflation can also benefit consumers. If the price of their house or the value of their investment portfolio goes up, the consumer has additional buying power also.

Cost Push Inflation

Cost-push inflation is a scenario where all around price levels go up, creating inflation. This happens because of rising prices in the important inputs of raw materials as well as higher wages for labor. This type of inflation appears because of rising production factors costs. This leads to a lower amount of total supply and production in the economy. With a smaller quantity of good being produced as the supply weakens while demand for such goods remains constant, the final cost for the finished products goes higher. This creates the inflation.

Cost-push inflation most typically begins when the costs of production rise. This is many times an unexpected cost increase. It could come as a result of higher prices in input raw materials, an unforeseen shutdown of or damage to a key production facility (like with natural disasters or fire), or forced higher wages for the employees in production. The higher wages could result from an increase in the minimum wage that automatically boosts the salaries of the workers who were making less than the new legally accepted minimum standard.

In order for such cost-push inflation to occur, the associated demand of the product in question has to stay constant while the changes in costs of production are actually happening. Producers then feel they have no choice but to compensate for the rising production expenses. They raise their end prices for their consumers so that they can hold their profit margins as they attempt to keep up production with anticipated demand for the products.

There can be several unanticipated causes of this cost-push inflation. Natural disasters are a common example. There might be earthquakes, floods, tornadoes, hurricanes, or other kinds of large “acts of God” events that interfere with some component in the production chain. These create higher costs of production. Natural disasters that do not lead to higher costs of production do not qualify as an example of this type of inflation.

There are other actions that can eventually cause rising costs of production as well. It might be a strike of the plant workers that happens because of failed negotiations in contracts. It could also result from a rapid change in government as often happens in developing countries. This might create an inability for the country to keep up its prior levels of production output.

There are similarly cost-push inflation causes that may be anticipated but are still unavoidable. Present regulations and laws can change. These changes may be foreseen. Despite this, there could still be no practical means of offsetting the resulting higher costs that come along with the changes.

Cost-push inflation is one of the two main types of inflation. The other kind is demand-pull inflation. This is the opposite form. In demand-pull, higher production costs force up the price of an individual service or good. With demand-pull inflation, the increase in demand happens even when production may not be boosted to cover the rising needs. In such cases, the costs of the product will go up because of the resulting imbalance that is created in the natural demand and supply model.

Council of Economic Advisers (CEA)

The President's Council of Economic Advisors proves to be an agency of the President's Executive Office. They give the President unbiased and non partisan economic advice for coming up with both international and national economic policies. This council is made up of three people of whom one is the chair. They use analysis of empirical evidence based on economic research to come up with their regular recommendations to the President. They gather the most esteemed information they can to help the President in putting together the critical national economic policy and annual report.

In 2016 the Chairman of this CEA was Jason Furman. The two members of the group were Jay Shambaugh and Sandra Black. Distinguished one time chairs of the group include former Chairmen of the Federal Reserve Alan Greenspan and Ben Bernanke and 2016 Federal Reserve Chairperson Janet Yellen. This council receives significant support from a number of staff members. Among their support personnel are staff economists and senior economists, research assistants, and a statistical back office.

Congress established this Council of Economic Advisors for the President with its 1946 Employment Act. In this act, the legislation called for three members whom the President would appoint. The Senate was to advise on selection and give consent on the final selection of these members. Members chosen for the CEA are to be recognized for their experience, training, and accomplishments in the field of economics.

Their purpose in greater detail is to consider and explain the economic developments to the President and to review the activities and programs the government establishes for economic appropriateness. They are also expected to create and recommend policies to encourage production, better employment, and higher purchasing power in a freely competitive economy. One of the three members the President is to appoint as Chairman for the council.

The council specifically has five different duties in the performance of their role. They have to help with and give advice for the Economic Report that the President's office prepares annually. They are instructed to collect information that is timely and accepted on the economic trends and developments in the U.S. They can then analyze and understand if the trends are interfering with attaining the stated Presidential policy. The group has to put all of this information together and turn it in to the President.

A third role is to consider the activities and programs of the government. The CEA is supposed to ascertain which of these activities and programs are helping to advance the policy and which are hurting it so they can let the President know.

They must also create and recommend policies for the President that help to develop and encourage competitive free enterprise. These policies should help to reduce and stop economic fluctuations and to improve national production, employment, and purchasing power.

Finally, the Council of Economic Advisors was set up to create and provide a range of reports and studies that have bearing on national economic legislation and policies. These are to be drawn up as the President requests them.

Every month the CEA prepares a report for the Joint Economic Committee of Congress. This is known as the *Economic Indicators*. In this publication there is information on income, gross domestic product, business activity, production, employment, prices, credit, money, security markets, international statistics, and the finances of the Federal government.

They also produce reports and fact sheets on a nearly every month basis that address a wide variety of economic issues. These reports and the speeches and testimony of the members of the Council of Economic Advisors are all available to the public on their official website.

Credit History

Credit history is an official record that shows the company or personal history of borrowing and paying back loans. This history provides business or personal identifying information, a record of credit that the individual or company has, and negative elements such as bankruptcies and late payments.

It describes how individuals use their money and finances. It lists out the number of credit cards, loans and other obligations, and bills that a consumer has. It keeps records of whether they pay these bills in a timely fashion. The credit history information is compiled as companies send in data on credit cards and loans to one of the three main credit bureaus. These are Experian, Equifax, and TransUnion. They act as the gatekeepers of credit history.

These companies compile all of this information on credit and bills into a file called a credit report. This credit report is the repository of all an individual's credit history. It contains a great deal of personal information that starts with the owner's name, social security number, and address. All credit cards and loans are itemized out and detailed. It states the total money a person owes. Finally, credit reports put together a profile on the individuals as to whether they pay their bills late or on time.

Credit history and credit reports are important for individuals. Businesses will not loan out money to people until they know all about them and their spending and borrowing habits and past. Businesses find all of this information on personal credit history in these credit reports and then make decisions as to whether they will extend credit in the form of a credit card or make a loan to the applicant.

Some employers choose to examine a candidate's credit report along with a job application. Insurance companies also consider it when they are determining rates of their customers. Even cell phone and utility companies often look it up when they are deciding how much a person will need to pay in deposits to start service.

Credit history is also used to create a credit score. Credit scores are numbers that the three credit reporting bureaus maintain for individuals using their credit history. If the credit history is good, then the credit score will be as well. Individuals can see their credit history and obtain their credit reports for free every year. Credit scores are not available unless people pay for them.

High credit scores convey a good credit history. Lower credit scores refer to a poor credit history for an individual. Each of the three credit bureau companies will have a slightly different score for a person. High credit scores range from 700-850. Low credit scores start from 300 to 600.

Credit history as shown in a personal credit report is very important to know. Each of the three companies is required to send individuals their credit report every year showing personal credit history on demand. Individuals are able to request this at no charge by going to AnnualCreditReport.com.

There are other companies that advertise offers to provide credit scores for free along with free credit reports. These are usually promotional offers that require individuals to sign up for a monthly service of some type in order to qualify for them. Such offers are often monthly credit monitoring services for a fee. As a rule, a person will generally have to pay something to obtain his or her credit scores.

Credit Ratings Agencies

Credit Ratings Agencies are those companies whose purpose is to consider and report on the financial strength which firms and government agencies demonstrate. They report on national as well as international corporations and agencies in this capacity. Their reports are most interested in the ability of the entities in question to fulfill their obligations for both principal and interest repayments of their bonds and other kinds of debts. Besides this, the various ratings agencies carefully examine and review the conditions and terms on every debt issue.

The end result of the agencies' work is to release a credit rating on both the debt issues in particular and the debt issuers more generally. When they agencies have high confidence that the issuer will be able to meet their debt servicing of principal and interest as promised, they will issue a high credit rating. When the opposite is true, the credit rating will be lower. It is entirely possible for a particular issue of debt to receive a differing credit rating from the issuer. This heavily depends on the particular terms of the issuer.

The impacts of these debt issue ratings are enormous in the industry and for the specific issuers in question. Those debt issues that obtain the best credit ratings will receive the most attractive interest rates from the credit markets. This is because the confidence of investors in an entity's capability of making their various payment obligations comes down to the credit ratings agencies review, analyses and especially ratings. Since the interest rates which investors demand for a specific debt issue will be inversely correlated to the borrower's particular creditworthiness, weaker borrowers will have to pay more while the stronger ones will enjoy paying less.

In this way, the credit ratings agencies act on behalf of businesses in much the same capacity as the consumer credit bureaus do for individual consumers. Such credit scores which the credit bureaus develop for individual people will greatly impact the interest rates at which individuals are able to borrow money.

The downside to these credit ratings agencies and their work is that they have been made the scapegoat for company and government defaults in recent years. Their research quality in particular has been the target of heavy criticism from observers and analysts who point out companies which they rated highly suddenly collapsed. Governments in Europe on which they provided high credit ratings defaulted or almost defaulted on their debts, as with Greece in particular.

This caused third party observers to argue that the various credit ratings agencies are actually poor at financial forecasting, at uncovering growing and negative trends for the debt issuers they follow, and also are overly late in revising down their ratings. Besides this, critics point to the many conflicts of interest of the ratings agencies. This is because the debt issuers are able to pick out and pay the ratings agencies for the reviews of their bonds. In a survey conducted in 2008, 11 percent of the various investment professionals surveyed by the CFA Institute responded that they had observed personally instances where the major ratings agencies had actually upgraded their given ratings on bonds when they were pressured by the debt issuers in question.

There are only three firms today which dominate the space, and this is part of the problem. The Wall Street Journal provided the ratings shares of the big 3 agencies in their 2011 report. Of the 2.8 million ratings they issue collectively (with the other seven minor agencies), S&P 500 controls the greatest market share with 42.2 percent. Moody's holds 36.9 percent of the market. Fitch rounds out the top three with 17.9 percent.

The article claimed that fully 95 percent of all revenues in this industry were earned by the big three. Only 2.9 percent of the ratings issued came from the other seven firms. The other seven credit ratings agencies were A.M. Best, DBRS, Japan Credit Rating Agency, Rating and Investment Info., Egan-Jones Ratings, Morningstar Credit Ratings, and Kroll Bond Rating Agency.

Between the top two issuers Moody's and Standard & Poor's, they provide ratings for roughly 80 percent of all municipal and corporate bond issues. They are typically regarded as a level higher than Fitch. One particular example speaks volumes. While Egan-Jones had downgraded the U.S. Federal government debt to the second highest rating years earlier, it was ignored largely by the markets and world. When Standard & Poor's took the same action by downgrading the Federal government of the United

States debt to AA+ on August 5th of 2011, this shook the world bond, currency, and stock markets. It demonstrates the clout S&P and Moody's especially enjoy over all of their various credit ratings agencies rivals.

Credit Report

A credit report is an individual or business' credit history. This includes their record of borrowing and repaying money in the past. It similarly covers data pertaining to any late payments made or bankruptcies that have been declared. In some countries, credit reports are also referred to as credit reputations.

When an American like you completes a credit application for a bank, a credit card company, or a retail store, this information is directly sent on to one of the three main credit bureaus. These are Experian, Trans Union, and Equifax. These credit bureaus then match up your name, identification, address, and phone number on the application for such credit with the data that they keep in their bureau's files. Because of this match up process, it is essential that lenders, creditors, and other parties always provide exactly correct information to the credit bureaus.

Such information in these files at the three major credit bureaus is then utilized by lenders like credit card companies in order to decide if you are deserving of having credit issued to you by the creditor. Another way of putting this is that they decide how likely that you will be to pay back these debts. Such willingness to pay back a debt is usually indicated by the timeliness of prior payments to other lenders. Such lenders will prefer to see the debt obligations of individual consumers, such as yourself, paid on time every month.

The second element considered in a lender offering loans or credit to individuals like you is based on your actual income. Higher incomes generally lead to greater amounts of credit being accessible. Still, lenders look at both willingness, as shown in the credit report and prior payment history, along with ability, as shown by income, in deciding whether or not to extend you credit.

Credit reports have become even more significant in light of risk based pricing. Practically all lenders of the financial services industry rely on credit reports to determine what the annual percentage rate and grace period of repayment of a loan or offer of credit will be. Other obligations of the contract are similarly based on this credit report.

In the past, a great deal of discussion has gone on considering the information contained in the credit reports. Scientific studies done on the issue have determined that for the most part, this credit report information is extremely accurate. Such credit bureaus also have their own authorized studies of fifty-two million credit reports that show that the information contained therein is right a vast majority of the time.

Congress has heard testimony from the Consumer Data Industry Association that in fewer than two percent of credit report issue cases have there been data which had to be erased because it was wrong. In the few cases where these did exist, more than seventy percent of such disputes are handled in fourteen days or less. More than ninety-five percent of consumers with disputes report being satisfied with the resolution.

Currency

Currency is also known as money that is accepted by businesses, the public, and the government as payment for goods and services. This includes paper notes and coins that a government issues and that circulate around a country and its economy.

Internationally, currency can be used to pay for imports in the balance of payments. Since ancient times currency has always formed the medium of exchange for trade. Currency has evolved over the years from gold and silver coins to bills that represent them to paper money that is today backed only by faith and trust in the government that issues it.

The U.S. currency has become the most heavily used reserve currency and medium for exchange around the globe. In the U.S., the BEP Bureau of Engraving and Printing creates currency in the form of the U.S. dollar. They produce literally billions of dollars of this currency every year and deliver them to the Federal Reserve System. These bills are known as Federal Reserve notes but are more commonly called dollars. The Federal Reserve states that there are around $1.4 trillion in these bills in circulation.

Keeping up with this incredible demand for dollars currency is not easy. The BEP proves to be among the biggest such operations for printing currency in the globe. They maintain operations in both Washington, D.C. and Forth Worth, Texas. Times have changed considerably at the BEP from its humble origins in 1862. In those days, they produced this currency on a machine that the small group of operators cranked by hand. They did this in the Treasury building basement.

Nowadays they utilize impressive technology that involves a cutting edged manufacturing process to produce the American paper money. The personnel doing this work are craftsmen who are extremely well trained and very skilled. They work with specific equipment and state of the art technology that utilizes the time tested historic techniques for printing. The production process involves a number of specific steps.

Counterfeiting has created a challenge for the BEP. They redesigned the U.S. currency to defeat the criminals who counterfeit the dollar bills. Special background colors have been added to these new notes that ensures it is harder to counterfeit their more secure safeguards. Such improved designs are used on the $100, $50, $20, $10, and $5 bills. These were rolled out in stages, with the new $20s brought out in 2003. New $50s followed for 2004, $10s for 2006, $5s for 2008, and the all new $100s for 2013.

The newly improved currency notes are the identical size as the prior issued notes. The images are historical with similar pictures to ensure that the bills appear and feel like other American dollars. Old security features are still utilized as well. This includes the watermark on the portraits that can be seen against a light, $5 special two number watermarks, a special security thread that can only be seen when placed to glow beneath an ultraviolet light, and better color shifting ink that shows different colors as notes are shifted.

$100 notes still have the raised printing and 3 dimensions security ribbons as in the last re-design. Counterfeit notes are still a tiny percentage of the circulating currency in the U.S. Technology advances have made it easier for computers to create realistic looking counterfeit notes.

Treasury has seen more of these computer generated fakes in recent years. This is why they chose to redesign the American paper currency so they could keep ahead of the technology empowered counterfeiters and their expanding methods for designing and printing the various dollar notes.

Currency Intervention

Currency intervention is also known as currency manipulation or forex intervention. These central bank-pursued interventions happen as they buy or sell their own national currency on the global foreign exchange markets. They do this to raise or lower the value of their currency.

Though these types of manipulations have occurred since the Great Depression, they are fairly new as a form of national monetary policy. Countries that have used this type of intervention heavily to limit the rise of their currencies in recent years are Japan, China, and Switzerland.

In general, central banks use currency intervention as a tool to contain the rising value of their own money as compared to those of other countries. When currency values appreciate, a nation's exports become more expensive and so are less competitive abroad. This happens because their goods cost more to buyers in their own foreign currencies. It explains why central banks prefer lower currency values which boost their nation's exports and improve economic growth rates.

The first significant use of currency intervention occurred on the side of the United States in the depths of the Great Depression. The American government counterbalanced imports of gold coming from Europe by selling off American dollars so that the gold standard would be upheld. Only when globalization had dramatically impacted economics did the large scale currency interventions of today become more commonplace.

China has been a major perpetrator of currency intervention in recent decades. They have been constantly concerned with keeping their Chinese Yuan value down against the dollar so that their all important exports did not become more expensive to their biggest customer. They aggressively sold Yuan and bought assets denominated in American dollars such as Treasuries in order to keep up a peg against the dollar.

The Swiss National Bank and Bank of Japan have also engaged in manipulation of the currency markets more recently to try to stem the over appreciation of their own national currencies. As the recipient of safe haven investment flows, these two countries find economic instability causes investors to seek their currencies the franc and yen for safety.

They have responded by selling their own currencies and buying those of main trading partners, such as the euro and dollar. Switzerland made headlines in January of 2015 when it suddenly abandoned its interventionist Euro ceiling as unsustainable. The Swiss franc gyrated as much as 30 percent higher in value in hours before settling between 10 percent and 20 percent more against the euro and dollar.

Currency interventions can be either sterilized or non sterilized. Sterilized interventions do not alter the money base of the country. Instead they offset foreign bond purchases or sales by performing the opposite transaction with its own currency bonds. Either means of intervening requires the central bank to sell or buy foreign currencies or bonds issued in such currencies. This allows them to decrease or increase their currency's value in global forex markets.

Central banks may also purchase and sell currency using transactions in forex spot or forward market instruments. They are literally buying or selling foreign currency with their own nation's currency in these cases. They pursue such actions in order to impact the near term valuations of their currency.

Economists question how effective such interventions really are. They generally agree that sterilized transactions cause little lasting effect. Spot and forward market purchases and sales tend to affect values short term but often do not last. Economists mostly concur that longer term currency interventions which are not sterilized can effectively impact exchange rates since they change the monetary base.

Currency Standards

Currency standards are the typical means for fixing a currency at a set rate nowadays. A Currency Standard means that the value of a currency is pegged to a stronger, more internationally recognized currency, like the Euro or the Dollar. These Currency Standards are similarly known as reserve currency standards.

Within the world reserve currency system, single national currencies actually assume the important standard, or role, that gold always carried for hundreds of years in the gold standard. Another way of putting this is that a nation would fix the rate of its proprietary currency to so many units against another country's currency. As an example, Great Britain might choose to fix its British Pound Sterling currency to the Euro at a real exchange rate of one pound equals one point twenty-five Euros. In order to keep this fixed rate of exchange, Britain's central bank, the Bank of England, would have to always be prepared to offer Euros for Pounds, or Pounds for Euros, upon demand for this set rate of exchange. The principal way that the Bank of England would affect this would be to keep Euros in its reserves against a day when a greater demand existed for Euros to be exchanged for Pounds on the world FOREX markets.

These currency standards stand in contrast to the gold standard. Under the long held, incredibly stable period of the gold standard, central banks instead held gold to back up and exchange against their own currency. Using the reserve currency standard, the same central banks instead keep a stockpile of the chosen reserve currency on hand. In whichever case, the reserve currency will be the one to which a given nation fixes its own currency.

The majority of nations that decide to fix their exchange rates will peg to one of two types of currencies. You might see them choose one of the main currencies utilized in international transactions for settlement. Alternatively, they could elect to fix their currencies to that of one of their major trading partners, which would also make sense for settlement purposes.

Because of this, you see many countries around the world peg their national exchange rate to the United States dollar, since it still proves to be the currency that is most widely held and traded around the world. As another fixing choice, the Euro is increasingly utilized for pegs. Fourteen different African countries which had all been French colonies in the past had set up the CFA, or colonies of French Africa, Franc zone. When they did this, they fixed their new CFA Franc to the French Franc.

After the French abandoned their Franc in favor of the newer continent wide Euro in 1999, the CFA Franc became pegged to the Euro. Another example is the Common Monetary Area of South Africa. Participating in this are Namibia, Swaziland, and Lesotho. These nations fix their currency against the South African Rand, the powerhouse currency of the South African continent, and their biggest trading partner by far.

Customer Base

A customer base refers to a company's prospective customers who the business might be serving. There are many individuals who believe this only pertains to the customers whom a business already counts. Still analysts tend to include in those customers who share common buying habits in the category. This is the case even when the customer has not come into the relevant store location or bought one of the company products yet.

In this group of all potential customers is a narrower set of the customers who are loyal followers of the company products. Business analysts call this group of consumers repeat customers. Business strategies focus on the critical need to turn every one-time customer into a repeat customer. Every company is interested in this, even when not all companies are focused on growing their entire customer base.

Theories on how to build up reliable and impressive customer bases abound. They run the gamut from offering periodic promotions to advertising the company products, brand, and services effectively to offering the highest possible customer service to clients. Any way a business manages to bring people into the store these are possible customers and could become a part of the reliable customer base. The hardest challenge is to bring them back to the store repeatedly.

It is well known that repeat customers are always the most crucial component of any businesses customer base and ultimately company success. These are the ones who will repeatedly and consistently spend money buying the business' products or services. They are also the best possible word of mouth advertising regarding the finest qualities of the company.

It is interesting to realize that some customer bases do not preexist at all. This is because some businesses provide a unique service that establishes a new customer pool which was not around before they began offering the service to the community. It happens when a company comes up with an idea to provide a service to people that they did not even realize they needed.

The trick for many businesses is to find a way to balance the differences between a company's end goals and the needs of the customer which will change periodically. Businesses have to be capable of adapting their strategies to the shifting requirements of a consumer base. At the same time, the business can not be spread in all directions simply chasing consumer fads.

The trick is to build up a loyal customer base which counts numerous repeat customers. When a business develops these types of customers, analysts call them an installed customer base. This refers to those clients of a company who are already utilizing the various products which the company produces.

It is helpful to look at a tangible example to better understand this idea. A company might sell laptop computers, printers, and software. The installed customer base would be only the customers who count at least one of the business' products working in their house. If they were interested in buying a laptop, they would be merely a member of the potential customer base for the business.

It is always more costly to add new customers than it is to keep those which are already existing customers of a business. This is why so many companies today focus their primary efforts on customer service, retention, and relations with their current customers. It does not take much in the way of advertising to keep an existing customer base. The good news is they already know the products.

This is why some promotions and occasional special pricing offers to loyal customers is enough to keep them coming back for more of the core business products. Companies often do this by maintaining as complete an existing customer mailing or emailing list as they possibly can. It is easy to send them promotions in the mail and even easier via emails.

Cyclical Manipulation

Cyclical manipulation refers to government interference in the natural economic cycles. This can lead to extreme booms and busts over the long run as governments attempt to prop up booms and forestall busts. Cyclical manipulation is mostly accomplished through the altering of government set interest rates. This is accomplished on a regular basis by the Federal Reserve Board in the United States.

Economic cycles as a concept are occasionally referred to as Business Cycles. This idea is one that explores the alterations in economic activity that change over time. Elements contemplated in explaining economic cycles are comprised of GDP growth, employment rates, and household incomes.

Within economic cycles, two main types emerge. These are booms and busts. Booms are commonly seen when a strong economy is operating. Busts, or recessions, are tied to economic growth that proves to be below trend. In the U.S., the NBER, or National Bureau of Economic Research, turns out to be the ultimate trusted source that gives out dates of troughs and peaks which actually make up economic cycles.

The NBER is part of this cyclical manipulation in the United States. The first step of the manipulation is the way in which they refer to booms and busts. They euphemize them as expansion or contraction. When a few portions of the economic data are getting better, then this is expansion, and when these same indicators are declining, it is called contraction. Such definitions focus entirely on the data movement, versus the historical norms.

Cyclical manipulation is accomplished principally through the changing of interest rates by the Federal Reserve. When the cycle is one of boom, or expansion, they attempt to cool the economy down to prevent inflation. They do this by raising the interest rates to slow down lending and spending. Unfortunately, as economic activity then slows, this leads to an economy that can then fall into bust, or contraction.

At this point, the Federal Reserve begins cutting the interest rates, sometimes massively, in an effort to stimulate the economy once more. As the interest rates fall, businesses and consumers borrow and spend larger sums of money. This gets the economy going once again. The irony of this cyclical manipulation lies in the fact that the very effort of the government to keep the cycles from becoming extreme leads to changes in the cycles that the Fed wishes to prevent altogether.

Economic Cycles Theory believes that even though these highs and lows average together to create an average trend economic rate of growth, this trending growth rate remains stable over time. The government through the Fed attempts to manipulate these cycles to keep the growth rate along these trend lines consistently. There has been no effort made in the Economic Cycles Theory to explain the economic activity levels in long running time frames of decline, but only in growth. This policy of only focusing on growth is yet another demonstration of the cyclical manipulation.

Debasement

When economists speak of debasement, they are referring to lowering the value of the money in an economy which is utilized to purchase goods and services. There are a number of ways that this can be done and has been accomplished throughout history. These include reducing the amount of precious metals in coins, eliminating the commodity backing, deficit spending, fractional reserve lending, and re-denominating a currency.

The practice of debasement by reducing the amount of precious metals in coins dates back to Roman times. The Imperial Roman government reduced both the amount of silver and the size of their denarius coins over time. They maintained the same denomination in the process. The silver coins began as nearly pure 4.5 gram pieces that finally had only two percent silver content left in them when they were replaced altogether.

The U.S. engaged in this same practice after 1964. Half dollars, quarters, and dimes had all contained 90% silver through that year. They were altered to clad coins with copper cores and a nickel copper plating beginning in 1965. This means they ceased to be commodity money and became Fiat money with value only because of government decree.

More recently, governments began debasing their currency by eliminating the currency's commodity backing of silver and gold. The U.S. Congress abolished the silver certificate legislation in June of 1963 and stopped redeeming bills for silver as of June 24, 1968. The gold standard that had backed up U.S. paper bills died in 1971 when then President Richard Nixon abandoned the currency standard unilaterally. The U.S. and other developed nations have been using Fiat currencies completely since then.

Deficit spending is another means of debasement. As governments print excess bills or issue debt to pay for their spending, the engage in this. The dangers of this practice are that as the money supply increases, so too does inflation. The U.S. money supply has been tripled using this means in the years of the Great Recession from 2007 to 2012. The runaway government spending has increased U.S. federal debt four fold from the years 2000 to 2016 (from $5 billion to around $20 billion total).

Governments can also use banks in debasement. This practice is known as

Fractional Reserve Lending. Banks are able to create money from thin air by loaning out significantly more money than they keep in reserves. Only a small percentage has to be kept on hand for the withdrawal of deposits. Money can be lent out versus kept on reserves to a factor of even ten to one. It leads to bank runs and bank panic if too many depositors attempt to withdraw all of their money at a time.

Currencies can be re-dominated by a government replacing an older unit of currency for a newer one. They do this by changing the currency's face value without allowing its foreign exchange rate to be altered. This re-dominating often causes hyperinflation. As bill values are changed by 10, 100, 1000, or even higher amounts, inflation can increase exponentially as well. When re-denominations became sufficiently high, the currency finally becomes worthless. This devastating result has transpired numerous times in history, most recently in Zimbabwe.

Debasing the Currency

Debasing the currency refers to the all too common historical process of lowering a currency's actual value. In the past, this phrase commonly came to be associated with commodity money made principally from either silver or gold. Should the sum total of silver, gold, nickel, or copper be reduced, then the physical money is called debased. Even venerable institutions like the Roman Empire, with a thousand year history of growth and stability, have stooped to such debasing of the currency.

Reasons that a government chooses to debase the currency in this way center around the financial benefits that the government is able to reap. These are done at the citizenry's expense though. Governments that lowered the quantity of gold and silver in their coinage found that they could quietly mint more coins from a given fixed quantity of metal on hand.

The downside to this for the general population centers on the inflation that this in turn causes. Such inflation is yet another benefit for the currency debasing government that then finds that it can pay off government debt or repudiate government bonds easier. The populace's purchasing power is significantly reduced as a result of this, along with their then lowered standard of living.

Debasing a currency lowers the value of the currency in question. Given enough time and abuse by the governing authorities, this debasing can even lead to a collapse in the existing currency that causes a newer currency or coinage to be created and launched for the nation or state.

In present day times, debasing the currency is accomplished in more subtle means. Since currencies these days are made of only paper, involving no metal, debasing the currency simply involves printing additional paper dollars. With the advent of electronic banking, even this printing press operation is no longer required. The government simply creates money on a computer screen, literally conjuring it out of thin air.

They are able to accomplish this in one of two ways. One way that they do this is via the Federal Reserve, which buys treasury securities by simply crediting the receivers' bank accounts with electronically created money. The Federal Reserve then has tangible assets in Treasury bills that is it able to trade or sell when it wishes.

Another way that this creation of money that debases the currency is able to be performed is through the Fractional Reserve Banking System. Since the Federal Reserve only requires banks to keep a ten percent reserve ratio of deposits on hand, these banks when they are credited funds from the Federal Reserve are able to loan this new money out in multiples that are equivalent to the leverage created by this ten percent only reserve ratio. In both of these ways, the Federal Reserve is able to create more money quietly and at will. This is how modern day debasing of the currency is effectively accomplished.

Debt Ceiling

The Debt Ceiling refers to an American budgetary and financial constraint which the nation self imposed beginning in 1917. Congress mandates this limit for the maximum amount of debt the Federal government may have at any point in time. Back on November 2nd of 2015, the U.S. Congress suspended the debt ceiling with the Bipartisan Budget Act of 2015. The ceiling remained suspended through March 15th of 2017, after the Presidential election. They did this deliberately to allow time for the new President (Trump) and his (Republican) Congress to establish themselves before they have to address the continuous debt crisis of the United States.

The prior debt ceiling was a whopping $18.113 trillion. Because the country was about to surpass this level on March 15th of 2015, then American Treasury Secretary Jacob Lew ordered a suspension to the debt issuance of the U.S. He began engaging in what analysts call “extraordinary measures” in order to stop the debt from breaking through the artificially created limit. To do this, he quit paying Federal government staff as well as the retirement fund contributions for U.S. Post Office employees. He began to sell the investments which these funds held as well.

The debt limit also covers a significant quantity of debt which the Federal government must repay itself. This includes the massive creditor the Social Security Trust Fund. Money owed to everyone outside of the U.S. government they call the American public debt. This amount represents approximately 70 percent of the aggregate Federal debt.

It was actually the Second Liberty Bond Act of 1917 which first saw Congress establish the initial debt ceiling. This law permitted the U.S. Treasury Department to sell Liberty bonds in order to pay for the then-vast costs of the U.S. military involvement in the First World War. By such an action, Congress gained the upper hand in overseeing total government spending for the first moment in U.S. history. Up to this point, the Congress had only held authority to approve particular debts, such as short term notes or for the Panama Canal.

By 1974, Congress found a way to gain absolute control over the budget process and effective spending in the United States. They called this new law the Budget Control Act of 1974. This new procedure for the budget envisioned Congress working closely in concert with the U.S. President to agree on what amount of money the country's government will actually spend. This all made the debt ceiling need irrelevant, since all it does is permit the Federal government to borrow necessary funds to pay for spending it previously approved anyway.

The reason this debt ceiling still matters is because Congress intentionally limits the amount of money which the U.S. Treasury may effectively borrow with it. If they do not continuously raise this artificially imposed limit, then the United States will default on its outstanding debt obligations. In general, the Congress has experienced no remorse for raising it. They raised it around ten times over the last decade, of which four of those times occurred in only 2008 and 2009.

This debt ceiling becomes a crisis in the event that both Congress and the American President are unable to come to an agreement on the country's fiscal policy. This has happened with alarmingly increasing frequency over the last few decades. It was an issue in 1985, 1995/1996, 2002, 2003, 2011, 2013, and 2015. The ceiling and associated government spending becomes an issue when the debt versus GDP ratio becomes excessively high.

The International Monetary Fund states that the maximum safe level for developed nations is 77 percent. After this point, holders of government debts then feel justifiable concerns that the nation will be unable to create sufficient revenues to repay the total debts.

Deflation

Deflation is simply the prices of goods and services going down in a given time frame. Deflation is the opposite of inflation, which is the rising cost of goods and services over a period of time. This does not make deflation a good thing in the long run.

Another way of defining deflation is the increasing value of money versus various economic goods over a span of time. With inflation, money is becoming less valuable versus goods over time. Deflation happens as a result of the interaction of four factors. On the one hand, the supply of money in circulation might decline. At the same time, supplies of available goods might increase. The need for goods could drop as well. Finally, the demand for money could go up. If any of these four things happen either separately or in concert, deflation is commonly the result.

The easiest way for deflation to occur is as the supply of goods available on the market goes up at a more rapid pace than does the supply of money. The combination of these elements explains how some goods' costs go up while the costs of others go down at the same time. Despite this, deflation can pose certain problems.

The majority of economists today concur that deflation proves to be both a symptom of economic problems as well as a malaise in and of itself. Some buy into the concepts of good and bad deflation. Good deflation happens as companies are consistently capable of manufacturing goods for cheaper and lower prices because of gains in productivity and other ways of reducing costs. This type of deflation permits a strong and growing GDP growth, with lower unemployment, and rising profits.

Bad deflation is more challenging to grasp. Bad deflation rises as a result of the central bank, or the Federal Reserve, choosing to revalue the country's currency. Or, you could say that the supply of money declining results in this negative form of deflation.

The actual problem that deflation causes is that it creates uncertainty for businesses and their relationships. As a rule, business thrives on confidence and falters on the unknown. Borrowers have to make loan payments that turn out to be greater and greater amounts of purchasing power in deflationary time periods. All the while, the value of the asset that you purchased with the loan is declining. In these circumstances, many borrowers elect to default on the loan and its payments.

A declining spiral similarly exists in deflationary periods. Since businesses begin to enjoy fewer profits, they decide to reduce their employment roles. Individuals do not spend as much money as a result. Businesses then realize smaller profits and again cut back. This degenerates into a vicious cycle down before long, as it becomes self reinforcing. Consumers learn that larger ticket items such as houses and cars will actually cost less in the future and then delay their purchases.

Though deflation has been discussed as a potential problem for the U.S. economy with the economic downturn, the reality is far different. At the same time, from 2006 to 2009, the Federal Reserve massively increased the money supply by more than three hundred percent. This argues not for deflation in the United States' future, but for inflation instead.

Deflationary Bias

Deflationary Bias refers to a government approach to managing inflation versus deflation. Inflation means that prices are rising, whereas deflation signifies that the prices of goods and services are decreasing. It is helpful to consider a real example of these two opposing concepts in order to understand them and the problems deflation can quickly cause.

If individuals go to their local grocery store and discover that bread has increased to $2.50 instead of the previous price of $2.00, they will not be happy. This is inflation and represents inflationary bias. On the other hand if the individuals went down to the car lot and discovered that a car which sold for $25,000 before is now selling for $23,000, they would be ecstatic. This is deflation and represents a deflationary bias. In general, consumers will always prefer deflation to inflation, at least on the surface.

The picture becomes more complicated when debt is considered. On a consumer level, as home prices decline, the home owners suddenly find themselves holding a mortgage that may be higher than the house's actual value proves to be. As this becomes a severe problem, individuals who own the house and are paying down the mortgage little by little (over likely 30 years) will not be able to sell and move simply because the mortgage is so much greater than the value of the house. The debt laden homeowners become unwitting victims of deflation in these cases. As a result, they are unable to move to expand their job hunting possibilities and will likely cut back on spending as they realize that they are upside down in the home thanks to the ravages of deflation.

This logic similarly applies to business as well. Because contracts exist in fixed terms not real terms, as real prices rise or fall, losers and winners emerge every time. As inflation occurs, sellers in a contract prove to be the winners, along with debtors whose debt is priced less in real terms. When deflation happens, prices fall and the sellers and debtors become the all around losers as their debt now costs more to repay in real terms. The buyers and creditors are the winners in this deflationary scenario. Ultimately this means that regardless of accounting tricks and confusing statistics, both deflation and inflation create income transfers with zero sum game losers and winners.

Governments attempt to smooth out the precarious extremes of either deflation or inflation utilizing monetary policy. The problem occurs as some prices rise at the same time as others fall. Gas prices may be declining at the same time as new cars are becoming more expensive. This is where the various monetary policies of governments meet their match. As these policies are effectively massive but blunt instruments, it is impossible for them to flexibly address the two extreme scenarios simultaneously.

This leaves policy makers with one of two unappealing choices. They will have to show one bias or another in their approach to managing an economy. Will they pursue an inflationary bias or instead a deflationary bias? With the inflationary bias they will be favoring greater employment levels and higher growth over the shorter term time frame. With a deflationary bias they will be favoring lower employment and less growth over the short term. The problem is that these biases similarly impact both sellers and buyers of any assets as they cause the assets to be less or more valuable in real terms as the debt in which they hold them is constant.

The reason that central banks and policy makers hate deflation so much is because of the real world effects on holders of debt. They are in terror of deflation since it alters consumer and business psychology and spending. With the Western societies that are so heavily indebted, deflation is the greatest possible enemy. This is true for the consumers, businesses, and especially the debt-ridden sovereign governments alike.

It is why the policy makers around Europe and the U.S. are desperate to re-inflate their respective economies. Japan has been caught in a deflationary spiral for decades now. The terrifying result has been a long period of economic stagnation and malaise from which they have never escaped since the end of the 1980s.

Demand Pull Inflation

Demand-pull inflation is one of the two types of general inflation. It comes because of powerful consumer demand in an economy. When many different people choose to buy the identical product, this will result in a price increase. If this scenario transpires in an entire economy on all kinds of goods, then it becomes the demand-pull type of inflation.

Keynesian economists utilize demand-pull inflation to explain the events when prices begin to go up from an imbalance of the relevant demand and the total available supply. When all around demand within the economy greatly overtakes the full supply, prices rise. Economists have colorfully called this type of inflation the unavoidable and unfortunate result of too many dollars chasing after an insufficient quantity of goods.

This Keynesian theory describes what happens when there is an increase in employment. It subsequently results in a growth in total demand. Because demand is rising, companies engage additional employees to help them boost their total output. The more individuals businesses employ, the higher employment goes. Finally, business output is insufficient to keep up with their demand so the total cost of the good will increase to match demand.

Demand-pull inflation should not be confused with the other kind of inflation referred to as cost-push inflation. In the cost-push variety, wages and prices go up together and transfer from one economic sector to another. The two types of inflation move in basically the same way yet work because of different causes.

Demand-pull inflation demonstrates the way that rises in price begin. Cost-push explains how it is hard to stop inflation after it has started. The main concept behind demand-pull inflation centers on powerful consumer demand which exceeds total supply to substantially drive higher inflation. All markets are limited to a specific quantity of goods. When the demand for the finite goods becomes enormous, the costs of the goods must rise to be higher.

Ultimately, demand-pull inflation results from five different causes. When spending increases from consumers, then businesses become confident enough to put on additional staff to keep up with demand. A second is when exports suddenly rise and this causes the relevant currencies to become undervalued. A third happens when government spending rises.

Another is the expectation and prediction of inflation causes companies to raise their prices to keep pace with it. Finally, too rapid growth in the monetary supply can cause such demand-pull variety of inflation. When there is an overabundance of money within the economy then there will not be enough goods to go around without prices rising to compensate and reduce the demand.

Oil refineries provide a solid example of demand-pull inflation. If they operate at full capacity, these refineries create this type of inflation. Regulatory issues from environmental concerns make it difficult for refineries to operate at full capacity. This limits the available supply of oil products. It is not that there is an insufficient amount of oil or companies producing it. Instead the problem results from artificially imposed legislation that keeps the market from receiving the ideal supply of finished goods that are in high demand. This causes the oil industry to be among the largest contributors to supply-demand inflation.

Depression

Depressions in economics are loosely defined as major declines in a country's GDP, or gross domestic product. The gross domestic product is made up of four major components. These include money that consumers spend, government spending for goods and labor, investment affected by government agencies and individual companies, and the net sum of the country's exported products.

All of these elements are combined to come up with the country's annual gross domestic product. Another simpler way of stating the GDP is in the counting of everything spent on services, goods, research, investments, and labor in the nation.

Depressions are then commonly said to happen as the country's GDP drops by minimally ten percent in only a year. There is not any consensus on the precise amount of decline in terms of percentage that must occur. Following the notorious stock market crash in 1929, the Great Depression that happened in the United States and throughout Europe demonstrated a sharp decline in GDP not only the first year but also over the following years.

In the months that came after this market crash, the U.S. GDP fell by in excess of thirty percent. After that it rose for a while, though not nearly to the pre-crash levels seen earlier in the U.S. This demonstrates the difficulty in simply defining depressions simply by looking at GDP declines and increases.

The Great Depression is mostly held to have continued until the very end of the 1930's decade. Real recovery nationally then did not begin until the outbreak of World War II in 1939. The reason that this is the case is that additional factors besides simply GDP declines have to be considered in evaluating what is and is not truly a depression.

The Great Depression had many negative characteristics besides simply falling GDP's. With plummeting industrial output, major numbers of jobs disappeared. As significantly smaller amounts of money came into workers hands, a great deal less could be spent on consumer goods or business investments. Without this money circulating back to businesses, firms were unable to hire workers back. The numbers of people dependent on help from the public assistance funds were greater. Job recovery did not materialize as hoped.

From time to time the Gross Domestic Product did rise in the 1930's. It never returned to the normalcy seen before the beginning of the Great Depression until the United States became fully involved in the Second World War. Demands for military equipment and weapons for the war did many things to help the American economy. Young men found employment in the army, industry suddenly had rising demand for military products, and job openings were more than the able bodied people available to fill them. At this point, women began entering jobs in industry in the place of men for the first time.

Nowadays, some respected economists worry that a depression like one not seen since the thirties could again be gripping the nation. This is because unemployment from the Great Recession remains stubbornly high, goods and services' prices are rising at a faster pace than payrolls in the majority of industries, and requirements for public assistance are higher than they have been since the end of the Second World War. The biggest fear today is that many of the jobs that are disappearing, such as technology and manufacturing, will never return, as they are migrating overseas to countries where workers are paid significantly less.

Devaluation

Devaluation involves an intentional adjustment to the downside for the currency value of a country. This is done in comparison to a currency standard, basket of currencies, or a single currency. This practice turns out to be a monetary policy tool for those nations that are either using semi fixed exchange or fixed exchange rates, like with China. Sometimes individuals confuse this tool with deprecation. The opposite of devaluation proves to be revaluation.

The government which issues the currency is the party that chooses to devalue it. Devaluations are always intentional, while depreciations instead result from activities beyond the scope of the government sector. A country has several motivations for devaluing its currency. The leaders might be attempting to fight against imbalances in their nation's balance of trade.

By devaluating, they make the national exports more affordable which helps them to compete more effectively in the global market place. It also makes their country's imports more costly for the citizens. This helps domestic consumers to choose to buy goods offered by their own domestic businesses. It strengthens the national economy.

It may seem like an appealing choice to devalue a currency. In reality, there are negative side effects to pursuing this option. When the leaders make the imports more costly, they protect their own native industry. These companies can then descend into inefficiency since they do not have much serious foreign competition any more. A greater number of exports as compared to imports also will increase the total demand. This often causes higher inflation at some point.

There are a number of different examples of official devaluations in the world. It may happen because of a variety of different reasons, yet government choices always lead to it. Egypt is a classic example. The country has long struggled with continuous strain from the black market demanding USD American dollars. This black market rose to prominence because of a shortage in foreign currencies that discouraged domestic and foreign investments in the Egyptian economy and also negatively impacted national businesses. The Egyptian government chose to put down the black market deals by devaluing their own Egyptian pound against the US Dollar by 14 percent back in March of 2016.

At first the Egyptian stock market delivered a favorable response after the currency devaluation. The black market reacted by depreciating the USD to Egyptian pound exchange rate. This caused the central bank to intervene. They were forced to announce a further devaluation of their currency again on July 12, 2016.

China also began to quietly devalue their currency throughout 2016. They did this in preparation for the U.S. presidential election results of November. Since both American candidates Donald Trump and Hillary Clinton were speaking out against the relationship with China, the country figured this would give them the opportunity to revalue their currency following the election in a move that would make it seem to be cooperating with the new administration. This makes the Chinese complicit in two rounds of currency devaluation, one to set up for the later intended opposite devaluing action.

Disposable Income

Disposable income proves to be the remaining income after an individual has met all of his or her income tax obligations. It is utilized as a means of ascertaining the health of an entire society, as well as a person's general economic condition. Disposable income also turns out to be among the main measurements for determining personal wealth.

Although they are sometimes used interchangeably, disposable income should not be confused with discretionary income. Discretionary income is simply any income that remains following paying the taxes and other customary living expenses. This means that the value for disposable income is a greater amount than discretionary income proves to be in practically every case. Still disposable income does not really deal with the day to day costs of living that people encounter in their normal lives.

For you as an American, disposable income typically proves to be anywhere from ten to fifteen percent of the personal income of an individual. All of the rest of the money goes into one of a number of different taxes. Naturally, this would be individually determined as a result of the amount of income that you have, the withholding allowances that you enjoy, and the state in which you reside. Similarly, for other countries, disposable income can be figured more or less by examining the typical tax rates.

Disposable income commonly decreases in difficult economic times, such as recessions and depressions. This does not happen because of an increase in taxes. Instead, it is more a factor of the likelihood of it falling in challenging economic times as companies cut back on employee payrolls. Because of this, lower disposable income will mean that people have more difficult times in fulfilling their present obligations. This will make them far less likely to take on new financial responsibilities.

When people do not make enough money to be taxed, then their disposable income may actually prove to be about the same as their total income is. This is similarly the case in nations that do not charge their citizens personal income taxes. In such cases, gross income and disposable income are identical.

Besides being used for spending on needs and expenses, it can also be saved and invested. Through wisely purchasing cash flow investments with disposable income, the resulting disposable income in the future can actually be consistently higher as regular investment income comes in to the person's account. Disposable income used for capital gains investments will commonly lead to one time gains on sales, which will only temporarily increase disposable income for one time.

Dollar Standard

The dollar standard came about as a result of the breakdown of the Bretton Woods agreement and international monetary system. In 1973 the U.S. (and then other developed countries) had abandoned the gold standard. The central bankers and finance ministers of the world could not reach agreement on a new standard for managing monetary relations and international trade. What emerged was a nameless new system that the nations did not officially consent to or sanction.

This de facto dollar standard received its name as the world moved away from gold as its main reserve currency and into U.S. dollars. Gold had underpinned the Bretton Woods system along with the monetary systems of the 19th century. The decision to move away from it as the ultimate backer for paper currencies had major implications for the world economy and trade.

The biggest result of the dollar standard was that it permitted the United States to finance unbelievably huge current account deficits and government spending simply by selling its trading partners and other countries its dollar denominated debt instruments. Under the previous Bretton Woods system and classical gold standards from past centuries, these additional imports that exceeded exports would have to be settled with gold.

The positive effects of this dollar standard are that it brought about globalization on a scale never before seen. This happened as the nations of the world were able to sell their goods and services to the U.S. on credit. It permitted economic growth to accelerate far more rapidly than would have been possible otherwise. This was especially the case for major swaths of the developing countries. It also served to keep interest rates and consumer prices extremely low in the U.S. Inexpensive manufactured goods could be produced with cheap overseas labor and then brought into the U.S. in dramatically growing quantities.

There are also three negative consequences of such a global dollar standard that may prove to be disastrous in the future. The first is that some international nations amassed enormous stockpiles of dollar reserves because of their financial account surpluses. This led to their economies overheating and their asset prices inflating enough to cause economic catastrophes. Asian Crisis nations and Japan are the most stunning examples of countries which suffered harm from these effects. These states escaped from the looming economic depressions thanks to their national governments taking on huge debt to bail out their banks which had gone bankrupt.

A second major problem is that the flaws of this dollar system have led to massive asset price inflation in the U.S. This resulted from America's creditors and trading partners choosing to reinvest their surplus dollars back into assets which were dollar denominated (especially stocks, company bonds, and real estate). This constant chasing of U.S. investible assets created bubbles in the American stock markets, pushed property prices throughout the U.S. to levels that were unnaturally high and not sustainable, and helped to misallocate corporate capital on an epic level.

Finally, the dollar standard's rapid creation of credit permitted nearly every industry to over invest. This has led to an overabundance of capacity and deflationary pressure which is reducing the profitability of companies throughout the globe.

Thanks in large part to the excess this new monetary system permitted, the U.S. economy is struggling under historically unprecedented debt burdens in government, corporate, and consumer segments. The world which finds itself overly dependent on exporting to the U.S. on credit struggles with difficult choices. They can continue the process even though they are fearful of overexposure to dollars and dollar denominated assets. They might also change dollar surpluses back into their national currencies which would raise the value of these currencies and hurt exports and overall growth. Some like China are pursuing a third way by acquiring as much gold as they can with their dollars, albeit slowly enough not to cause a rush for the dollar exits.

Dow Jones Industrial Average (DJIA)

The Dow Jones Industrial Average, commonly referred to by its acronym DJIA, is also many times called the Dow 30, the Dow Jones, the Dow, or even just the Industrial Average. It proves to be the second oldest stock market index in the Untied States after the Dow Jones Transportation Average. The Dow Jones Industrial Average came into being when Charles Dow, the co founder of Dow Jones and Company worked with a business colleague Edward Jones, a statistician, to come up with an index that monitors the industrial sector. This index demonstrates the daily stock market trading session progress of thirty of the largest companies that are publicly traded within the U.S.

Ironically, most of the present day thirty companies listed in this index no longer have much or even anything to do with the historical definition of heavy industry. The components in the average are weighted by price and scaled in order to adjust for the impacts of stock splits and varying other forms of adjustments. This means that the total value that you see in the daily representation of the Dow Jones does not prove to be the true average of the different company stock prices.

Instead, it is the total of such company prices that are added up and then divided by a special divisor. This divisor is a number that is adjusted any time one of the company stocks underlying it pays a dividend or engages in a stock split. In this way, the index presents a constant value that is not altered by the external factors of the component stocks.

The Dow Jones Industrial Average remains one of the most heavily followed and carefully watched indices in the American stock market, along with peers the S&P 500 Index, the NASDAQ composite, and the Russell 2000 Index. The founder Dow intended for the index to monitor the American industrial sector's actual performance. Even so, the index is constantly affected by much more than simply the economic and corporate reports issued. It responds to both foreign and domestic incidents and political episodes like terrorism and war, as well as any natural disasters that might cause economic damage.

The Dow Jones Industrial Average's thirty components simultaneously trade on either the New York Stock Exchange Euronext or the NASDAQ

OMX, which are the two largest American stock market outfits. Derivatives based on Dow components trade via the Chicago Board Options Exchange, as well as with the Chicago Mercantile Exchange Group. The latter is the largest futures exchange outfit on earth, and it presently owns fully ninety percent of the Dow Jones founded indexing business, along with this Industrial Average.

Investors who are interested in gaining the ability to track the progress of the Dow Jones Industrial average have several choices. There are index funds that buy the components of the index so that you do not have to own all thirty companies yourself. You might also invest in the Dow 30 by purchasing shares of the Exchange Traded Fund known as the Diamonds ETF. This trades under the AMEX exchange via the symbol DIA. Finally, you could by options and futures contracts based on the performance of the Dow Jones Average on the Chicago Board of Trade.

Econometrics

Econometrics refers to the utilization of math and statistics in the discipline of economics. Economists include these branches of study in order to test their hypotheses and theories. They attempt to predict future trends by employing it. The idea is to consider economic models and test and re-test them by using statistical trials. They finally contrast and compare the ultimate results against known real-world examples. This is why economists often divide up the study into the two groups of applied and theoretical.

Economists work econometrics by merging math, economic theory, and statistical hunches. Through these combinations they are able to analyze various theories. They harness a variety of tools including probability, frequency distributions, regression analyses, statistical inference, times series methods, and simultaneous equations models.

It is always helpful to consider a real life example to understand a difficult concept like Econometrics. Economists might choose to work this discipline in order to consider the idea of income effect. Many economists will theorize that individuals who boost their income will also expand their spending levels. The way they can test out such an economic hypothesis so that it becomes proven and accepted is with the tools of this discipline. These include multiple regression analysis and frequency distributions.

The field of Econometrics became discovered and advanced by the three renowned economists Ragnar Frisch, Lawrence Klein, and Simon Kuznets. The lot of them received the Nobel Prize in economics for their achievements and work with this discipline of economics.

Utilizing Econometrics in practice is not as difficult as it might at first seem. Step one is to consider a data set so as to come up with a particular hypothesis. This must give reasons for the shape and nature of the data. In such a first step, the variable which the employing economists will consider they must specifically define. Relationships between independent and dependent variables must also be detailed. It is this stage of the discipline which depends enormously on the economic theories to be tested for their usefulness as the study progresses.

In the next step, the economists will have to select their particular statistical model or tool with which they will test out the economic hypothesis. For a model to be considered effective, it will have to outline particular relationships mathematically between the dependent variables and the variables which explain them in the given test. The most typical tool economists use is the multiple linear regression model. It is because they consider this to be the most practical tool in the discipline. The reason for this is that the relationships can be expressed in a linear fashion. It is appropriate to many situations since the most typical relationship between data sets proves to be linear. All that this means is that a change in one variable will lead to another positive correlation with the other variables.

A third step revolves around entering in all of the data set information to a software program specifically created for econometrics. Such a program will utilize the economist chosen statistical model in order to tabulate the preliminary results. It employs the entered economic data to come up with these results.

Finally they come to the most critical (and also coincidentally last) step for proving a hypothesis using Econometrics. The economists in question gather the program's outputted results and prepare a real-world type of test. It is this test that gives the economist the knowledge regarding the validity of the model that was proposed and tested. For the model to be useful, it must deliver reliable and accurate predictions which can be back tested and so proven. When the economists uncover the results they anticipated, then they know that their hypothesis is in fact a theory. Should the results not be what they anticipated, additional inferences or other hypotheses will be required.

Economic Commission for Latin America and the Caribbean

The Economic Commission for Latin America and the Caribbean is a key United Nations body which is referred to by its various acronyms of UNECLAC, ECLAC, and the Spanish acronym CEPAL. This regional commission of the U.N. has a mandate to foster economic cooperation between the various member states.

There are 45 member nations in total. This includes 13 in the Caribbean, 20 in Latin America, and 12 which lie outside the region. There are also 13 members who are associated but not full members. This is because they are territories which are not independent (such as the United States Virgin Islands), commonwealth of the Caribbean (such as the Cayman Islands), and associated island countries. The ECLAC produces a number of valuable statistics which cover the nations in the area. It also makes cooperative forms of agreements pairing up these nations and nonprofit organizations of the world.

The Economic Commission for Latin America and the Caribbean arose in 1948 at the behest of the United Nations. It was originally called the UNECLA UN Economic Commission for Latin America. In the year 1984, they passed a resolution in the United Nations to bring in the nations of the Caribbean into the organization's name. This commission is under the ESOSOC UN Economic and Social Council and reports to them.

The current executive secretary of the Economic Commission for Latin America and the Caribbean as of 2017 is Alicia Barcena Ibarra of Mexico. She has served since July of 2008 in this head leadership role.

There are several important locations of the Economic Commission for Latin America and the Caribbean. Its headquarters lie in Santiago, Chile. There are two sub-regional headquarters as well. These are the Central American head office in Mexico City, Mexico and the Caribbean head office in Port of Spain, the capital of Trinidad and Tobago.

Other important country offices exist in four nations. These include Buenos Aires, Argentina; Montevideo, Uruguay; Brasilia, Brazil; and Bogota, Colombia. The organization also maintains a liaison office in Washington D.C. in the United States.

The member states of the Economic Commission for Latin America and the Caribbean include Venezuela, Uruguay, the United States of America, the United Kingdom, Trinidad and Tobago, Suriname, Spain, South Korea, St. Vincent and the Grenadines, St. Lucia, St. Kitts and Nevis, Portugal, Peru, Paraguay, Panama, Norway, Nicaragua, the Netherlands, Mexico, Japan, Jamaica, Italy, Honduras, Haiti, Guyana, Guatemala, Grenada, Germany, France, El Salvador, Ecuador, the Dominican Republic, Dominica, Cuba, Costa Rica, Colombia, Chile, Canada, Brazil, Bolivia, Belize, Barbados, Bahamas, Argentina, and Antigua and Barbuda.

The associated members of the Economic Commission for Latin America and the Caribbean are the United States Virgin Islands, the Turks and Caicos Islands, Sint Maarten, Puerto Rico, Montserrat, Martinique, Guadeloupe, Curacao, the Cayman Islands, The British Virgin Islands, Bermuda, Aruba, and Anguilla.

It was the creation of this Economic Commission for Latin America and the Caribbean that became an instrumental part of the so-called “Big D development.” Economists and regional historians blame the founding of this ECLA and the subsequent policies it recommended for the ensuing problems including dependency and structuralism. This is because though the group was established in the period following the Second World War, its roots in fact date back to the era of colonialism which saw the European powers such as Britain, France, and Spain and the United States as economic overlords of much of South America.

It was the League of Nations which came up with the idea for a need to economically restructure South and Central America and the Caribbean. Stanley Bruce drew up the document which he presented to the League of Nations in 1939. This had a major impact on the establishment of the United Nations Economic and Social Committee in the year 1944. At first the ECLA did not have effective policies for Latin America.

In subsequent decades though, it dramatically altered the balance of economic power in the region as member nations became prisoners of the interest and principal repayments on loans for development projects. These were forced upon them by the World Bank, IMF, and the Economic Commission for Latin America and the Caribbean.

Economic Embargo

An Economic Embargo is a type of government-mandated order. They limit the exchange of goods and commerce to a country which they specify. Sometimes they affect only particular goods which represent a threat to the importing nation's vital economic or security interests.

Such embargoes are typically established because two nations find themselves in a political spat or economic disagreement or because of a combination of the two. The idea behind such an economic punishment and restriction is to economically isolate a nation. The enforcer hopes to make life difficult for the people and ultimately government of the nation so that it will have no choice but to carry out the desired actions of the embargo issuer.

There are two different main forms of economic embargoes. A strategic embargo will stop the trade in any type of military hardware, equipment, or goods with the victim nation. Trade embargoes are far more restrictive. They stop any individual or company from exporting given goods (or sometimes all goods) to the nation which is targeted. In today's world, a large number of countries depend on global trade to function and prosper. This is why an economic embargo can prove to be such a potent weapon to influence the behavior of a nation without having to go to war.

A trade embargo may lead to severe negative consequences for the victim nation and its economy. The U.S. often relies on the mandates issued by the United Nations in deciding which countries to inflict economic and trade embargoes against. In many cases, allied nations will combine their collective economic and trade powers to issue joint economic embargoes. This restricts trade with the targeted countries in an effort to force them to make strategic changes for world peace or to engage in better humanitarian behaviors.

The United States has become famous for its imposition of a few long-lasting economic embargoes against other sovereign states. Among these are ones which have been in place on nations that include Iran, North Korea, and Cuba. Back in the decade of the 80's, a number of countries with the U.S. enforced a trade embargo against the once-prosperous nation of South Africa. They did this because of several issues the combined governments opposed, including apartheid (segregation and official discrimination against the native African black population by a ruling white minority) and a drive for nuclear technology and weapons capability within the country.

America- enforced embargoes leveled against some of these and other nations particularly leave out the trade of certain goods, such as necessary items. In these cases, they focus more exclusively on weapons, ammunition, and weapon systems or luxury item goods. Other forms of trade they leave in place. Comprehensive forms of economic embargoes are more devastating to the victim nations since they stop all types of trade between the victim nation and the inflictors.

After the terrorist attacks which began with September 11, 2001, American-led embargoes have increasingly tended to focus on threatening nations like the Sudan. This country and others such as Iran are well-known for their historic and present-day ties to terrorists and their funding around the globe. This makes them a direct threat to American national security interests and those of its allies and friends around the world.

The U.S. has occasionally also been the recipient of such economic embargoes. During the 1970s, the American economy suffered great harm because of the infamous Arab Oil Embargo. The Organization of the Petroleum Exporting Countries, or OPEC, enforced this oil embargo and created misery through skyrocketing gas prices, fuel rationing, and even gasoline shortages at the pump.

In the United States, it is the American President who has full authority to inflict embargoes in war times. This he can do under the existing Trading with the Enemy Act. Besides this, the President may also rely on the existing International Emergency Economic Powers Act to enforce national emergency based commercial restrictions. Such embargoes become administered by the Office of Foreign Assets Control within the U.S. This is a division of the Department of the Treasury that helps to find and freeze the ultimate sources of funds for both terrorist operations and drug businesses.

Economic Globalization

Economic globalization turns out to be an either hated or praised global phenomenon. It means that the economic picture and scenario for any given nation is dependent significantly upon the involvement of other often-time competing nations. A great number of countries who are friends supply resources to one another which the other countries simply lack.

Such resources can include imported technology, products, raw materials, services, and individual labor. Many critics have astutely observed that this process will eventually lead to closer integration and finally a one-world government, as has been gradually occurring within the European Union. This idea entails a centralized single government for all countries under one flag.

A popular engagement under the auspices of economic globalization is international trade. In this activity, countries exchange essential and luxury services and goods between one another. With countries that possess abundant natural resources, they rely on this system of trading to sell their unique resources so that they can improve their national economic situations.

International trade such as this has gone on for many centuries. The Silk Road which connects Asia and Europe in ancient trade demonstrates this. A modern day example of such international trade proves to be the toy industry. In this business, numerous toys sold in the United States and Europe carry the phrase “Made in China” upon their surface.

Economic globalization pertains to both economics and finances for countries, but it also impacts cultural identity and national politics as well. Tax treaties and trading policies are fashioned between various nations in order to protect either state from threats like terrorism or to control their trade. Multinationals can actually alter a nation’s appetite for foods. Corporations such as McDonald’s have managed to shift the eating preferences of consumers in Asian countries that believe rice should be the mainstay in their daily diets. European fashions from Paris, London, and Milan have managed to influence the styles and tastes of Asian and American consumers who import them to sell in their clothing shops.

It is easy to view economic globalization through either advantageous or disadvantageous lenses, depending on the perspective of the person judging it. The positive side effects are that it provides additional job opportunities and sometimes offers greater salaries. This often leads to faster and more economic growth and eventually an increasing standard of living. Such international cooperation has also fostered greater and longer periods of international peace between countries. It has further led to better cultural exchange through understanding and awareness of other cultures and countries. Technology has played an outsized role in this capacity.

Critics of economic globalization have much about which to vocalize their complaints as well. Many critics have successfully made the case that the disadvantages substantially outweigh the benefits. One negative issue is that it helps countries to burn through global natural resources on a larger and faster scale. This is a result of the higher demand for scarce raw materials which has grown with many developed and developing countries alike.

A second downside is that it enables human rights violations. Numerous nations are able to more easily exploit labor of other countries' populations when they are developing countries. Still other critics from the developing world point to how economic globalization is basically a disguised means of richer countries colonizing those which are poorer and less powerful. They do this by seizing control of the overall economic picture of the poorer countries. Regardless of how critics or fans view this economic globalization, neither camp is able to deny the amount of impact which it continuously has on the global development of today and for the foreseeable future.

Economic Growth

Economic growth represents a boost in an economy's ability to create and produce services and goods. This is compared from one period of time against another. There are two ways to measure this phenomenon. It may be quantified either in real or nominal terms. When real terms are used, economists have to adjust them for the effects of inflation.

Historically and routinely, total growth in an economy is determined and expressed in the form of either the old standard of GNP Gross National Product or the more recent standard of GDP Gross Domestic Product. There are also other infrequently utilized metrics for measuring growth in an economy.

The simplest way to express such economic growth is by utilizing total productivity. Gains in productivity often correspond to an increase in the average marginal productivity. In other words, the typical worker within a specific economy becomes more productive as the economy is growing. Economies may also obtain growth even without such an average marginal productivity increase. This happens when there are more births than deaths (higher birthrate) or as additional immigrants come into an economy and begin to work. It can also result from technological revolutions. Examples of this are the Industrial Revolution, the computer revolution, or the Internet revolution.

It is always true that economies experiencing economic growth will be able to produce a higher quantity of services and goods than they did before the growth transpired. Yet there are those services and goods which command a higher value than competing goods or services. Examples of this abound. Smart phones or laptops are considered to have a higher value economically than bottles of water or a shirt. This is why growth in an economy is effectively figured up by measuring the total value of goods and services which the economy produces instead of simply the quantity.

An additional dilemma comes as different consumers put varying values on identical services and goods. For example, for residents of Alaska an effective heater would command a higher value than it would for residents of southern California. Similarly, in Florida efficient air conditioners have greater value than they do in Canada. Other individuals prefer fish to steak, or steak to fish. Value is always subjective. This is what makes measuring the value of all goods and services challenging. It is ultimately why the current fair market value is what economists employ to determine value for the purposes of measuring economic growth.

Interestingly enough, only a few means exist to create growth economically. A relatively straightforward one is through the uncovering and exploitation of better or newly discovered physical economic resources. Before gasoline was discovered to have the ability to generate energy, petroleum had very little economic value. Gasoline and hence petroleum began to create economic growth once this discovery was made. This was true for those countries with an abundance of petroleum they could export as well as for countries that utilized the gasoline to more effectively move goods across their nations.

A second means of producing economic growth is by increasing the size of the labor force. When every other factor is equal, a greater number of workers will produce additional services and goods. Much of the impressive economic growth in the United States through the 1800s came from a constant inflow of productive and inexpensive immigrant labor.

The third means of creating such growth is by developing better capital goods or higher technology. Such capital growth and technological improvements are closely correlated to the level of business investment and savings. Both are needed for firms to pursue a significant amount of R&D, or research and development.

The final method for boosting economic growth lies in better specialization of labor pools. In other words, the workers have to increase their skills at their crafts. This boosts productivity because of extra practice or through experimenting with new or improved methods. Investment, savings, and specialization are the easiest to control and most reliable means of increasing the growth in an economy.

Economic Inequality

Economic Inequality concerns disparity financially between various groups of individuals. There are no societies in the world where all people fall into precisely the identical class economically. In other words, all individuals do not have the same amount of material or financial resources. Unfortunately, just the opposite is more common.

In many nations, some people have such vast income and wealth differences from others who live in dire poverty. On the other extreme, the wealthy live ultra luxuriously. This causes great and intense debate as the effects of economic inequality spill over into other parts of life that would normally not be determined by one's economic standing.

In most economies and countries, there are poor people, rich people, and then many medium classed ones which live in the middle. This is most clearly demonstrated in respect to the richest class. They earn and possess substantially greater resources than all of the other classes, particularly versus the bottom one. It is this whole scenario that economists call economic inequality.

Two different focuses surface as analysts consider such economic inequalities. Wealth is the first of these. This refers to the quantifiable amount of money and possessions that people have. Such wealth massively affects the lifestyle of individuals as it is almost exclusively the determining factor of what people can buy and what choices they have in their daily lives and when making longer-term plans. The wealthy naturally have higher standards of living than the rest of the classes.

The other critical financial indicator for measuring the level of economic inequality has to do with income. There are a number of individuals who possess no or little wealth as they have next to no meaningful income. In most cases, the people who command the greatest amount of wealth and so enjoy the highest standards of living are similarly the ones who enjoy the most significant levels of income.

It is interesting to realize that this kind of inequality economically is more severe in some nations and regions than it is in other ones. Nations that do not have sufficient social services find that the disparities are greatest and painfully obvious. In some of these countries, some individuals are extravagantly wealthy while others on the other extreme live in appalling conditions or suffer from starvation or at least severe malnutrition. Other countries have adequate social service networks and find that the gap between the richest and the poorest proves to be less severe. This still will not stop significant differences from appearing between the different groups and their actual lifestyles.

The debate rages on regarding economic inequality because of a variety of reasons. One strong argument against wealth and income disparities is that these dramatically impact the ability of citizens to obtain core services and basic items that ought to be easily available to all people. This includes such things as food, clean drinking water, legal representation, and adequate health care. Another complaint regarding inequality concerns the unfair access to impacting the political environment that the rich enjoy.

In recent years, the United States has been ranked among the most unequal of all developed nation rivals. In fact the OECD ranks the U.S. as second highest in inequality levels once it takes market incomes and adjusts them for the redistribution impacts of income transfer programs and tax policies (like unemployment compensation and Social Security payouts). According to their measurements, only Chile has a greater level of economic inequality from all 31 developed nations.

Similarly, the U.S. economic inequality has become the highest since 1928 in recent years. As of 2012, the highest earning one percent in the U.S obtained 22.5 percent of all pretax income. The bottom earning 90 percent enjoyed only 49.6 percent of the national income share.

Economic Indicators

Economic indicators are bits of economic data generally pertaining to the macroeconomic larger picture economy. Investors utilize them to decide on the investing climate as they consider the all around state of the economy. There are many different economic indicators which the government usually releases. Five of the most important are gross domestic product, consumer price index, employment indicators, PMI manufacturing and services, and central bank minutes.

Gross Domestic Product is the dollar value of every good and service a country produces in a set amount of time. It can be delivered in real and nominal formats. Real GDP makes adjustments for changes in the value of money. This indicator is one of the most anticipated by financial markets for its importance. Increases in GDP indicate an economy that is growing. Declines in it demonstrate an economy that is slowing. National growth rates like this are often utilized to judge the affordability of a country's sovereign debt. They also determine if companies operating in the country are likely to be profitable.

Consumer Price Index is an inflationary figure. It looks at the household purchased goods and services and measures their changes over time. This statistical estimate is compiled by taking prices from a group of representative items. This CPI is often used to discern how much inflation is. Markets watch CPI figures to determine if inflation is getting too high. When there is higher inflation it causes interest rates to rise and lending to decline. Deflation causes more lending and better interest rates. Inflation reduces the relative value of a currency and is bad for savers.

Employment determines the citizens' wealth and economic success. This makes employment indicators like unemployment and payroll data, income trends (earning more or less), total labor force, and percentage employed telling. These numbers are particularly important in developed countries that see most of their national income created by consumer spending. Declines in consumer spending often lead to an increase in unemployment. This in turn feeds into lower GDP numbers.

PMI manufacturing and services is part of the Purchasing Manager's Index. Markit Group developed this with the Institute for Supply

Management. They survey businesses every month to learn about business purchasing manager's activities in acquiring input goods and services. The most crucial of these surveys are the PMI Services and PMI Manufacturing indices. These are considered to be important leading economic indicators. When demand for business products declines then companies will decrease their buying of raw materials instantly. This gives a picture of problems in an economy long before consumer spending or retail sales figures will.

Central banks play such an important role in any nation's economy that their releases are very important. Markets study every word that comes from central bankers to learn what is in store in the future. Central bank minutes prove to be the official information releases that give out useful commentary on the economy and signal what actions the central bank will take in the future.

The United States has the Federal Reserve. It provides its well known beige book. In this book are economic conditions related anecdotally by each of the branches of the Federal Reserve Bank. These types of notes are also released by a great number of other central banks. Among these are the Bank of England, European Central Bank, and Bank of Japan. They are released publically on a routine schedule. Central bank minutes releases also give a clue as to when the group will raise or lower the national interest rates which affects everything from consumer and business lending activity to savings deposit rates.

Economic Occupancy

Economic Occupancy refers to the rate of paying tenants for an apartment building or some other rented out space like an office building. The managers and owners of apartment buildings and complexes commonly measure their success with both physical and economic occupancy rates. While these two concepts are related, they are not exactly the same. With physical occupancy, this pertains to the percentage of the total apartments (or commercial office suites) that the owners successfully rent. The rate of economic occupancy describes how many of these tenants are actually paying rent. The economic assessment speaks volumes more than the physical occupancy rate, since ultimately the economic one explains the apartment complex of office building's financial performance.

Another way to think of economic occupancy pertains to the percentage of rents which the owners and managers successfully collect from their tenants as measured against the total sum of money which could physically be collected. This ultimately describes how successfully or unsuccessfully management is optimizing potential revenues.

A number of reasons present themselves for why a building's unit might not be paying rent. The simplest explanation is that the units could be vacant. There are also gaps which exist from when one tenant leaves a unit until another finishes moving into the unit. Some buildings or complexes will find they need to offer discounts to lure in tenants. This might be half off the first rental month costs. Other tenants could depart while still owing the management company rents or fees. Many times, the manager of the apartments, maintenance head, or security guards will live rent-free on the property as part of their benefits as well. The downside is that while it is useful to have such key personnel living on site, it lowers the revenue stream on the property every month.

Figuring up the true economic occupancy is simple. This requires the property manager to divide the actually collected rent by the potential maximum collectable rent if every tenant paid the full price. It helps to consider a real world example of the concept. For any complex that possess 20 occupied apartments which rent for $1,000 per month, perhaps 16 actually pay the rent for one reason or another. This would amount to $16,000 divided by $20,000 for an 80 percent rate. Yet the physical occupancy would amount to a full 100 percent in any case. The best case scenario is to have as close as possible an economic occupancy as physical occupancy rate.

The measure for economic occupancy has various helpful applications. It demonstrates any complexes or office buildings which are suffering from serious issues. If the rate is low, then problems exist with either rent collection, tenant turnover, or both. It may mean that the complex or office building management is inadequate or the base of tenants is unable or unwilling to pay their rent because of property problems. Low rates of occupancy eat into the ability to pay operating costs of the property. Ultimately they mean that profits will be lower or outright losses will be present instead.

Realtors often use the economic assessment over the physical occupancy rates when they are attempting to value an apartment complex or commercial office building. Those properties which are losing money display an inability to retain their tenants. It is also important to compare apples to apples with this measurement. Calculating the economic occupancy on a week by week basis will show a bias of high economic results the final week of the month and a low result the first week of the month. This is why realtors will prefer to have the occupancy calculated economically on a month by month basis, as it filters out the discrepancies of weekly fluctuations.

Economic Output

Economic output refers to the amount of goods and services which a nation, industry, or company creates over a set time period. These might be utilized in later stages of production, traded, or otherwise consumed. The idea surrounding national economic output is a critical one in the world of economics. This is because economists opine that it is not enormous quantities of money which truly make nations wealthy, but rather their national output amount.

Other phrases that analysts and economists often use interchangeably with economic output include output and gross output. This should not be confused with GDP Gross Domestic Product. Value which is added on a national scale is the definition of GDP ultimately. On a local level, this is often called gross regional product or even gross area product. While the two ideas of GDP and output bear some similarities, they are not identical. Both concepts do measure the productivity economically of a particular nation or region for a given time period.

Economic output itself quantifies the total value for all services and goods. The problem with this idea is that it involves a double counting of all intermediate purchases. Looking at an example of this dilemma helps to clarify the issue at hand. If a furniture maker purchases its wood directly off of a saw mill at $150, they might then increase the value of it to $450 by creating an article of furniture. The output involved would be measured as $600. This represents all value in every sale involved for this particular chain of economic activity. The problem is that this method includes the wood value two times. It becomes doubly counted when it is the intermediate stage good and again in the final price or value for the article of furniture.

GDP on the other hand concentrates on only the services' and goods' additionally added value. Another way of defining this lies in the economic output minus the intermediate inputs included. When economists take out the goods' value which already came through the market once before, it allows for a more accurate assessment regarding the output. The strict GDP formula is then GDP equals the gross output minus the intermediate inputs. In the example above with furniture, the GDP equaled up to merely $450 because the formula takes out the $150 in wood inputs from the final sales price of $600.

In the real world, the overwhelming numbers of companies produce products which they make utilizing many materials that go through a few different suppliers hands in the production process. Each supplier will add its own value. Only in the end would this value be tallied into the cost of the ultimate product. The important take away from this is that there is a significant difference between GDP gross domestic product and economic output.

One of the great economic questions of all time that economists wrestle with pertains to why the national output for a given country will constantly fluctuate, sometimes dramatically. There is no one easy answer on which economists have consensus opinion unfortunately. Instead, economists generally concur that there are a variety of factors which cause output to rise and fall. With growth, the majority of economists can agree on there being three principal sources of economic growth.

These are labor increases, factors of production efficiency increases, and capital increases. This is a two-edged sword though. Growth to the factors of production inputs can also be negative. In fact when any factor leads to a decrease in the efficiency of production, capital, or labor, then the growth rate will subsequently decline. This finally translates to a drop in economic output as well as in GDP.

Economic Participation

Economic Participation refers to the labor rate of participation. This means that it measures the total active population participating in the labor force. Another way of saying this is that it pertains to the numbers of individuals which are actively seeking out work or who are already employed. The two categories are important to consider, as in economic recessions a number of active labor force workers will despair of finding a job and simply give up the search for employment. This means that the Economic Participation rate will decrease as this happens.

Such an Economic Participation rate is a key measurement to utilize when considering a body of unemployment statistics. This is because it reveals the numbers of those individuals who show interest in being a part of the active work force. Such people either have a job or are actively looking for one. They usually must be considered from 16 to 18 years of age or older to be eligible for inclusion in the category. Those individuals who are not physically capable of working or who lack the interest in working will not comprise the participation rate. This includes retirees, imprisoned people, students, and homemakers or stay at home moms.

This is an important metric to consider alongside the official unemployment rates. The reason is that many individuals who are called unemployed might not really be true participants in the active work force. If analysts only contemplate the unemployment rate by itself, they might arrive at the conclusion that a greater number of individuals are not bringing home income.

This does not meant that they are not actively contributing to the level of the economy. It might be that such individuals choose not to work for a variety of reasons. They could be spending retirement savings, building their skills as college or university students, or spending their spouse's earnings as stay at home moms. It explains why both unemployment statistics and the Economic Participation rate should be reviewed together to fully appreciate the true employment picture of an economy and country.

This Economic Participation rate becomes even more critical to understand when recessions bite. As an economy goes from reasonably good to particularly bad, many workers will simply give up looking for work after many months unemployed. At this point, they could simply abandon the workforce. The labor participation rate would then decline. The reason is that these individuals would no longer be classified as actively looking for employment. This explains why in recessions, sudden plunges in the labor participation rate would be carefully considered and evaluated.

A case in point is the effects of the Great Recession on the ongoing Economic Participation rate. The labor force impact from this worst economic collapse since the Great Depression of the 1930's proved to be absolutely devastating. The recession officially began in December of 2007. Per the NBER National Bureau of Economic Research, the unemployment rate stood at 5 percent that month. When the recession officially ended in June of 2009, this unemployment rate reached 9.5 percent and then climbed on to peak out at 10 percent by October of 2009.

In the eight years since then, the unemployment rate has nearly touched five percent again. Yet the labor participation rate has never recovered from the Great Recession. Many economists believe that this devastating recession and global financial collapse caused the acceleration of structural changes in the labor force participation rate. The rate has ranged from 67 percent back in 2006 to today's near 62 percent in 2017.

The decrease in the economic participation rate has been broad based and consistent since 2009 in fact. Many baby boomers decided to retire early as their job opportunities suddenly evaporated. Many individuals used government grants and loans to go back to university or college. Some women stopped working to be stay at home moms as the job opportunities were so scarce.

Economic Sanctions

Economic sanctions turn out to be both financial and commercial penalties which a nation or several nations level against a targeted nation, organization, or individual. Such sanctions can cover different types of punishments. Among these are tariffs, trade barriers, or financial transacting restrictions.

What is interesting about these is that they are not always applied thanks to an economic dispute. In fact they can be forced on other countries, organizations, or individuals because of several different types of military, political, or even social concerns. Such sanctions are often utilized to realize international and sometimes domestic policies or goals.

These economic sanctions may be deployed as an extension of international foreign policy. They are typically forced on smaller and weaker nations by one or more larger and richer ones because of two different reasons. It might be the weaker nation is actually a threat to the greater nation's security, as with Iran's aggressive nuclear weapons program versus the United Nations. It might also be that the more powerful country feels the weaker state is practicing human rights violations on its own people, as with Syria versus much of the rest of the world's countries.

This is why economic sanctions might be employed as a means of forcing the stronger countries' wills on the lesser one. Some of these policies pertain to achieving more open and fair free trade or for punishing and stopping violations of basic human freedoms and rights. In modern times, these forms of sanctions have often been utilized in lieu of waging actual military conflicts in order to reach desirable end results and outcomes without actual loss of human life.

The problem with these sanctions according to many analysts and economists is that they mostly harm the ordinary citizens of a nation rather than its government or military-industrial complex. Besides this, these kinds of sanctions are not always effective in achieving their hoped for results. Regime change is a classic example of this type of foreign policy. Though it is the most common basis for such sanctions, it is rarely successful.

Haufbauer et al. have studied these types of sanction policies and determined that in only 34 percent of the relevant instances did they work out successfully. An analysis of this study by Robert A. Pape ended with the conclusion that in only five out of the forty claimed successes did the results really stand out, which dropped the successful rate down to only four percent.

The reason for this is governments have a wide range of choices for trading partners and even financial conduits which they may go through. Consider the case of Iran and its frightening nuclear weapons program. For most of a decade the democratic nations of the world united to force a range of restrictive economic sanctions via the United Nations on the Islamic Republic. The sanctions were never one hundred percent effective, as countries including North Korea, Cuba, and Venezuela still continued to trade freely and openly with Iran. Some multinational companies and even a few countries secretly conducted trade with Iran as well.

The world's largest international bank (according to balance sheet) British multinational giant HSBC is the best known example of a company cheating on these specific economic sanctions. The United States' justice department found the banking giant with significant operations in 71 countries and territories guilty of helping the Iranian government to circumvent the international sanctions regime. While HSBC received several billion dollars in penalties, this did not reverse the damage to the sanctions' policy that they had already done.

These economic sanctions similarly impact the national economy of the country which imposes them to a lesser degree. When they erect restrictions on imports, the country imposing them will find its consumers suffer from less selection of goods. As export restrictions occur, the companies from the imposing nation(s) lose their access to and investment opportunities in the victim country. Other rival companies from foreign nations will take over these opportunities instead.

Economic Surplus

Economic surplus relates to supply and demand. They are also referred to as total welfare. There can be two different types of such economic surplus, consumer surplus and producer surplus.

A consumer surplus happens when a given product or service's price proves to be less than the greatest price level consumers would be willing to pay. This is something like an auction. Buyers go in to an auction with a maximum price amount that they are willing to pay.

Consumer surplus transpires when these buyers can obtain the product for a lesser price than their limit. This reflects a gain. Oil product prices are a real world example of potential consume surplus. When the costs for a gallon of gasoline decline to a lower amount that the consumers typically pay, the consumer realizes a profit in the form of an economic surplus.

Alternatively, a producer surplus happens as companies are able to sell their goods for more than the lowest price at which they were willing to sell. Using the same example of an auction, the auctioneer or house might have a minimum reserve on an item where they begin the bidding. The house will not accept lower than this price. They would realize a producer surplus if the auctioneer obtains a higher price than the reserve limit for the product.

This happens when the buyers keep bidding on the price of the item and thereby increase the price of the good until someone finally wins and buys it. The producer realizes more money than initially expected in this example of economic surplus. It is important to realize that producer and consumer surpluses are effectively zero sum gains. This means that the benefit of one is the loss to the other group.

There are side effects from either type of economic surplus. With a consumer surplus, this will lead to an eventual shortage in the producer's supply. This is because supply at that price simply can not stay abreast of the demand. People like to purchase additional quantities of any product available at an attractive price point. Alternatively, a producer surplus will result typically in an overabundance of supply. This is because prices are too high for consumers willingly to purchase much of the given product.

Economic surpluses happen because of an atypical disconnect between demand and supply on a certain product. It could also result if some consumers are ready and able to pay a higher price for a good or service than are others. If instead prices were fixed on the product while all consumers anticipated paying the same price, then shortages and surpluses would not exist.

In the real world this rarely occurs. This is because different businesses and consumers have various price points at which they are willing to sell and buy. In selling items, the competition is constant to produce the most and best product for the greatest value. With prices rising and falling because of demand and supply, surplus happens on the side of the producer or the consumer.

When demand becomes too great for a given product, the vendor providing the cheapest price will sell out. This leads to general market price increases, or producer surpluses. Similarly, prices will decline if supply is high and demand is insufficient, leading to a consumer surplus. Surpluses commonly arise if the product price is set too high at first at more than consumers will pay.

Egalitarianism

Egalitarianism refers to a philosophy that believes in some type of equality. The main idea behind it is that all individuals should be regarded and dealt with as equals, at least pertaining to political, religious, social, economic, or cultural equality. The tenets of egalitarianism hold that every human being has an equal moral value or basic worth.

It can be used as a political philosophy that claims that everyone ought to be treated as an equal, provided with the identical economic, political, civil, and social rights. It could alternatively be a social philosophy that pushes for the decentralizing of power and the breaking down of economic barriers between different people. Some individuals believe that this egalitarianism is the natural form of society.

Egalitarianism deals with the studies pertaining to social inequality. Unequal societies lead to many of the world's great social problems. Among these are infant mortality, homicide, teenage pregnancy, obesity, incarceration rates, and depression. A comprehensive type of study that was performed on the major economies of the world showed that a strong connection exists between all of these challenges in society and issues of social inequality.

Egalitarianism exists in numerous different forms. The most typical basis for it arises from political, religious, or philosophical backgrounds. Political precedents of egalitarianism date back to the Age of Enlightenment in the 1700's. At this time, modern government founders referenced egalitarian principals of morality that they lived by, such as the American concept of certain inalienable rights endowed to them by their Creator. These were laid into the modern framework of countries like the United States and France.

Religious egalitarianism is heavily rooted in Christianity. This Christian egalitarian world view states that the Bible is the basis for the common equality of men and women, as well as every economic, racial, ethnic, and age group. This comes from Jesus Christ's example and teachings, as well as other lessons taught throughout the Bible.

In philosophy, egalitarian ideas grew in substance and practice over the last two hundred years. Various sub-philosophies have arisen from this general philosophy, including communism, socialism, progressivism, and anarchism. Each of these concepts favored political, economic, and legal versions of egalitarianism.

Some of these egalitarian philosophies have gained significant and wide standing support with both the general population as well as the intellectuals in numerous countries. This does not mean that such ideas are actually put into universal effect though. On the other hand, democracy does involve many ideas of egalitarianism, at least in the political sphere. Representative democracy proves to be the ultimate realization of such political egalitarianism. Critics of this idea say that even though votes are given out on a one vote per one person basis, the actual power still rests with the ruling class and not the common people.

Elastic Demand

Elastic Demand refers to a factor of demand which is affected by the price. When the quantity of a good demanded responds substantially based on a change in the price or another factor inherent in demand, then the demand for the good in question is said to be elastic. When prices for a good or service decline even a little, consumers will often purchase a significantly greater quantity of the particular item. When prices instead go up a little, the consumers will typically cut back on their purchases while they wait on the prices of the good or service to return to the prior level.

When services and goods feature elastic demand, this describes items which the consumers are happy to comparison shop around for a more attractively priced substitute. The reason for this truth is that the buyers are not desperately in need of having the given item. This could be because they do not require it each day, or because there are many similar comparable choices which may be offered at more advantageous prices.

It is actually the laws of demand which lead the correlation between quantity purchased and price per item. This law claims that the price of an item is inversely related to the amount which consumers will purchase. As prices go higher, it is human nature for individuals to purchase fewer items. Elasticity of demand describes by how much the item quantity they purchase will drop as the price rises.

Where goods and services are concerned, there are actually two more kinds of elastic demand. Both of these quantify how the numbers purchased will specifically change as the price declines. These are inelastic demand and unit elastic demand. Inelastic demand simply means that the amount of the goods or services which consumers demand will change less radically than the associated price will. Conversely, unit elastic demand means that the amount of a given good or service which individuals demand will alter at the same percentage rate by which the price varies.

To figure out the elastic demand formula, one simply takes the quantity demanded percentage change and divides this figure by the price percentage change. Demand is said to be elastic as the percentage change of the quantity which consumers demand is greater than the associated price change percentage. This would mean the ratio is higher than one. As an example, if demanded quantity increased by 10 percent as the price declined by an associated fiver percent, then the ratio would be .10 divided by .05 for a total demand elasticity result of 2.00. It would mean that the demand was highly elastic.

Another scenario which may result is called perfectly elastic demand. This happens if and when the demanded quantity increases to infinity as the price declines by any percentage amount. Of course in the real world this is not possible. It does serve to illustrate the point that elastic demand possesses a ratio higher than one.

Conversely, inelastic demand is present as the demanded quantity increases by a smaller percentage than does the drop in price. Consider this example. When the quantity demanded increased by two percent as the associated price dropped by five percent, then the ratio proves to be .02 divided by .05. The result is .40 demand elasticity, which is under one. This means the demand is inelastic, and the item can not be easily substituted or replaced by the markets.

Unit elastic demand is present as the demanded quantity varies by exactly the same percentage amount as the price change does. This would mean the ratio proved to be exactly one. The example with this base case is easy to understand. If the demanded quantity rose by five percent as a result of an associated five percent decline in the price, then the .05 divided by .05 would yield a result of one.

Emerging Markets

Emerging markets prove to be those countries of the world that possess business and development activities that stand in the midst of fast paced industrialization and growth. Today, twenty-eight different emerging markets are considered to exist around the globe. By far and away the largest of these are China and India. The largest regional emerging market today is the ASEAN-China Free Trade Area that began operating on the first of January in 2010.

The concept of emerging markets dates back to the 1970's, when the term used to refer to these particular markets was LEDC's, or less economically developed countries. The comparison alluded to their levels of economic development as compared to the U.S., Western Europe, and Japan. Such emerging markets were supposed to offer higher risk levels for investors as well as the opportunity to make greater profits.

As this term had a slightly negative connotation, the phrase emerging markets replaced it. Some have claimed that this newer term is deceptive, since no one can be assured that a given country will actually migrate from less developed to a more substantially developed one. This has generally proven to be the case, but there are exceptions. Argentina has occasionally digressed from more to less developed.

Numerous examples of these types of emerging market economies exist, since twenty-eight different ones are labeled. These include countries that are grouped in more advanced emerging economies, such as Brazil, Mexico, Taiwan, South Africa, Poland, and Hungary. The secondary emerging economies are as follows: China, India, Chile, Colombia, Egypt, the Czech Republic, Indonesia, Morocco, Malaysia, Peru, Pakistan, Russia, the Philippines, Turkey, Thailand, and the United Arab Emirates. This list is compiled and occasionally updated by the FTSE group based in London, Great Britain.

In the last few years, several competing terms have arisen to challenge the emerging markets phrase. One of these is that of rapidly developing economies that refers to emerging markets like Chile, Malaysia, and the United Arab Emirates. All of these nations are experiencing torrid paces of growth.

The biggest of the emerging markets have earned their own acronyms in the past several years as well. Chief among these are BRIC, signifying Brazil, Russia, India, and China. BRICS includes the above four nations along with South Africa. BRICM is the original four BRIC nations and Mexico. BRICET signifies the first four BRIC members plus Turkey and Eastern Europe. BRICK includes the original four nations of the BRICK along with South Korea. Finally, CIVETS is comprised of Columbia, Indonesia, Vietnam, Egypt, Turkey, and also South Africa. Although none of these countries are particularly aligned by policy or ideology, they are currently gaining a more important role within the overall world economy, as well as in international politics.

For an investor who wishes to invest in these economies, there are several different investment vehicles available to them. Among these are both Exchange Traded Funds and Mutual Funds. One of these is the iShares sponsored MSCI Emerging Markets Index ETF with a symbol of EEM. Another is the iShares run MSCI EAFE Index ETF that has a symbol of EFA. Though these funds' prices can be up spectacularly in good years, they can also experience precipitous declines in periods of instability, such as during the worldwide financial crisis of 2007-2010.

Entrepreneurs

Entrepreneurs are individuals who have new business ventures, enterprises, and concepts. They take on substantial responsibility for both risks inherent in these as well as their end results. As such, entrepreneurs prove to be unique people for many reasons.

For one, entrepreneurs have trouble working for other people, even though they do work on behalf of clients. They will put all of their assets and money at risk because they have a driving passion to watch their endeavor expand. As a result of this, they occasionally have a couple of failures to their credit along the way. These individuals enjoy putting in the extra time and effort in the procedures of strategizing, modifying, amending, and adjusting their businesses. They are not afraid of long hours and constantly working when everyone else has given up and gone home for the day.

Entrepreneurs must have vision and foresight. They are required to see their enterprise not only as it is now, but also as it will look in a year from now, and two years, three years, and even five years to ten years in the future. This involves understanding what the process of the business will tangibly look like, not necessarily the employees who change from time to time. This is essential for any entrepreneurs to be successful in reaching their end goals.

Entrepreneurs are loners in a very real sense. They stand by themselves with their vision that only they can see so clearly. They are also alone in having the drive and passion to see their endeavor through. They understand that no one else in the business will care about it like they do, since no one else possesses the dream.

Very few people are entrepreneurs. It takes a hardy individual to be one. This is evident when you consider that the number of new businesses that go down in only the first year is fully seventy-five percent, mostly a result of insufficient commitment from the founder. Ninety percent of such businesses have folded by the conclusion of the second year for a variety of reasons including funding difficulties, family problems from working all of the time, and challenges in dealing with employees. Entrepreneurs are capable of overcoming these types of problems using their determination and energy.

Entrepreneurs are also those who invest money and have the risk of losing it. Many times they will act as venture capitalists and pour money into firms that have not long been operating. When you purchase items cheaply and sell them dearly, this makes you an entrepreneur on a smaller scale too. In the end, entrepreneurs are those who are willing and able to utilize their money in order to make more money.

Similarly, entrepreneurs are born leaders. They know what they want, and understand what to do in order to achieve it. They dream big dreams, form important ideas, and come up with concepts and opportunities. These leaders who are willing to engage in financial risks are true entrepreneurs.

European Debt Crisis

The European Debt Crisis refers to the ongoing European sovereign government struggle to repay various national debts the countries ran up over the past several decades. There were five of the peripheral EU states in particular that were unable to create sufficient economic growth in order to make possible their repaying of the national bondholders as they promised to originally.

These countries included especially Greece, Portugal, and Ireland, but also enmeshed were Spain and Italy to one degree or another. Though only these five nations showed signs of potential default during the crisis peak in the years 2010 to 2011, the crisis had broad and dangerous consequences that impacted not only the rest of the European Union, but also the world in general. The governor of the Bank of England called this the "most serious financial crisis at least since the 1930s, if not ever," back in October of 2011.

The European Debt Crisis did not suddenly appear overnight, but was years and even decades in the making. Slower growth from the time of the American based financial crisis and Great Recession from 2007 to 2009 demonstrated that many spending policies in Europe and the world at large were truly unsustainable any more. Greece became the poster child for the effects of reckless overspending in the following years. The Greeks had spent with great largesse for seemingly endless years and avoided painful but urgently needed financial and fiscal reforms. They were the first to feel the negative effects of weaker ongoing growth as it so happened.

As growth slows down, tax revenues also decrease apace. This means that greater budget deficits become impossible to sustain. The Greeks had been hiding the amounts of their large and increasing national deficits for years, but by the end of 2009, it was no longer possible to keep them from world markets and the enraged Greek populace any longer. The Greek debts had become so vast that they substantially exceeded the entire economy of the smaller nation.

Investors in their sovereign debt naturally retaliated by insisting on larger yields on their Greek national bonds. The unfortunate side effect of this action was that the interest payments on the Greek debt also skyrocketed, causing their debt burden to become so onerous that they could not manage it any longer. The EU and European Central Bank had to come riding to the rescue of the Greek government and economy in consequence. This did not stop investors and markets from pushing up the yields of bonds in other similarly indebted nations throughout Europe, where they expected similar crises and potential collapse as had already tragically occurred in Greece.

The vicious cycle of higher demand yields leading to greater borrowing costs for the nations in crisis led to greater fiscal strain which caused investors to require still higher interest yields on the troubled European sovereign bonds. This gradual erosion of investor confidence did not stay focused on Greece, but impacted the other shaky economies of Portugal, Ireland, Cyprus, Spain, and even G7 trillion-plus dollar economy Italy. This became known as financial crisis contagion. Portugal, Ireland, Cyprus, and Spain were forced to seek out bailouts either for their embattled sovereign government finances, their national primary banks, or in the cases of Portugal and Ireland, both.

The problems were exacerbated by the fact that the European Union moved so slowly to address the severe problems. This is because their actions required the approval of all 28 countries in the economic and political union. Bailouts were offered to the troubled governments via the European Stabilization Mechanism or ESM. The European Central Bank acted in a substitute capacity by cutting interest rates and providing unlimited loans to European national banks which were in trouble in exchange for assets (which were highly questionable at best) as collateral.

The problems of the European Debt Crisis are far from over fully five long years later. Italy's banks have not yet addressed their over $360 billion in bad loans to this day. Their third largest and oldest bank Monte Dei Paschi Di Sienna has 28 billion Euros in bad debts it has been trying unsuccessfully to offload as it sought out 5 billion Euros in fresh capital from skeptical investors. Greece is on its third consecutive bailout program from the EU so far in only five years. Portugal, Ireland, and Cyprus have all emerged successfully from their bailout and bank recapitalization programs, while Spain is on the right track and making measurable and material progress in escaping from theirs.

European Union

The European Union proves to be both an economic and political cooperation and block. It is made up of 28 independent European countries. There are several common representative institutions that bind the nations together. The European Council is a body that represents the various national governments. The citizens are represented by the European Parliament.

The common interests of the Europeans are represented by an independent group called the European Commission. These three bodies democratically legislate particular issues of mutual interest to the countries that belong. Most of the countries in Europe participate in the European Union in some form. Three countries that have opted not to are still associated members of the European Economic Area. This includes Norway, Iceland, and Liechtenstein.

Several European countries established the EU following the Second World War and its devastation. They wanted to encourage better economic cooperation and ties. The philosophy behind this was that countries which traded more closely shared an economic interdependence. This would make them less likely to engage in future wars and conflicts.

The group they created out of this philosophy in 1958 became the EEC European Economic Community. France, Belgium, Luxembourg, the Netherlands, Germany, and Italy were founding members that pledged to work towards closer economic cooperation and ties. Over the years since then, more and more nations joined to form an enormous common market.

The original economic union has increased its powers and scope to become a political union as well. As a result of this, they changed the name from European Economic Community to European Union in 1993. These areas of political cooperation include security and external diplomatic relations, migration policies and justice, health, climate, and the environment.

All aspects of this political and economic cooperation stem from the rule of law. Every action the EU takes is authorized by treaties that are democratically and voluntarily agreed on by the member nations. This is evident for member states in the institutions the Council of the EU and the European Council. Citizens themselves have their representation at the European Parliament.

The EU is able to boast of some significant accomplishments. It has ensured over fifty years of peace, prosperity, and stability on the continent. The organization has increased living standards throughout Europe, though not uniformly. Countries in the north and center have seen greater economic benefits and improvements than those on the periphery.

The EU also successfully launched the world's second most important reserve currency the Euro. These achievements received official recognition in the year 2012. That year the EU received the Nobel Peace Prize for its work in moving forward the democracy, reconciliation, peace, and human rights throughout the continent.

Benefits that EU citizens receive in the group have to do with freedom of movement. Removing the border controls between EU countries ensured individuals were able to travel without restrictions around the vast majority of Europe. They are allowed to work and live in the other EU countries as well.

This benefit extends to not only people, but also to goods, services, and money which are allowed to move freely back and forth as well. This has been a main economic advantage that the EU provided for decades. The EU also is working to come up with common cooperation in knowledge, energy, and capital markets to provide the optimal benefits from these to the various EU citizens.

The United States provided a diplomatic Mission to the EU since 1961. Both the EU and U.S. maintain close strategic ties and work together extensively. These issues extend from global problems like nuclear non proliferation to counter terrorism efforts. The EU has major investment and trade relations with the United States as well.

Export

The word export refers to a good or service that is sold and shipped out of a country. In business and economics terms, an export can be any kind of commodity or other good that is utilized in trade and transported out of one nation into another nation. These must be done in legal ways to qualify as exports. The opposite of the word export is the word import.

The word export is originally taken from the idea of shipping such services and goods out of the port of a given country. This made it an item that was sent literally “ex” port. This term came from the time when practically all international trade proved to be conducted via shipping.

Sellers of services and goods are known as exporters. These individuals are based in the exporting nation. The party who receives the goods or services in the overseas country is known as an importer. In the realm of international trade, exports means vending goods and services that are manufactured in the producing home nation to markets in other countries. Once these goods are received by the importer in the foreign country, they are offered to the consumers in the foreign country by distributors and domestic producers.

When a person or company wishes to become involved in exporting commercial amounts of goods, then they will have to become engaged with the customs entities in both the exporting home country and the importing receiving country. Smaller quantities of goods are exempt from such customs departments, particularly when they are of low individual value. This is why the rise of auction sites and other online retailers vending to international customers, such as e-Bay and Amazon, have managed to side step the customs departments in the majority of countries. This does not exempt small value export items from the legal rules and restrictions that are applied by the exporting nation.

A nation’s exports can be many different things in practice. Resource rich countries like Australia or South Africa will commonly export big ticket natural resource items like gold, oil, natural gas, uranium, or diamonds. Agricultural countries such as the Philippines and Honduras export rice and bananas to other countries in the world. The main exports of industrial countries such as Germany and Japan are instead final manufactured product goods like cars and machinery.

Some items may not simply be exported to every nation. They are subjected to export control. Export control involves Federal laws and rules that forbid the exporting of some information and commodities without a license. This is done to protect certain trades or because of sensitive issues related to national security. Specifically, the government might be worried about the final destination country or group that will receive the goods, such as Iran or North Korea. They may fear what the actual use of the export will be, such as equipment for enriching uranium. Sometimes, exports have capabilities that will allow them to be used for possible military applications that the government wishes to control and supervise, like with missile technology.

Federal Debt

The federal debt is also known as the national debt. This represents the entire dollar value of the money which the U.S. federal government has borrowed from its various creditors over the years. Creditors to the government are made up of all governments, businesses, individuals, and other national and international entities which own the debt instruments of the U.S. government.

This national debt has resulted from numerous government deficit budgets where they spent more than they earned in revenues. It is important to realize that this federal debt never includes any of the money owed by municipal or state governments, companies, or individuals. Instead it is the total of all federal government outstanding obligations. This figure contains not just the money the federal government originally borrowed. It is also made up by the interest amounts that it has to pay back with the borrowed funds.

Governments fall into debt when they are not able to bring in sufficient revenues to pay for their expenses on a variety of government programs. This includes military spending and domestic programs such as retirement benefits, Medicare, welfare, and constructing bridges and roads. Revenues are derived from a number of sources. These are made up of personal income and corporate taxes as well as government fees on things like passports, cigarettes and alcohol, and national park admissions fees.

For 2016, the national debt had risen to an enormous amount of greater than $19 trillion. As a percentage of GDP this is over 105%. It has rapidly increased from the years 2006 to 2016, as in 2006 the debt came in at less than half as much at $8.4 trillion. This represented only 66% of the national GDP at the time. Because of this dramatic and ongoing increase, the debate is always heated regarding what should be done with the national debt. Many individuals and observers like the Congressional Budget Office feel that the debt needs to be paid down. Others argue that the debt proves to be a needed catalyst to keep up economic growth.

The debt has come from successive increases in the federal government's annual budget deficit. These annual deficits represent the amount of additional money the government spends over what they take in for receipts. All of these deficits combined together plus interest paid equal the national debt.

When investors see the debt grow higher and anticipate that there will be greater levels of inflation, they become concerned about the value of their debt holdings. Some economists have conjectured that the government only intends to inflate away the value of the debt over time. This is why debt holders can ask for higher interest rates when they make future loans to governments they suspect of inflating away their debts.

Federal surpluses can be used to pay down the federal debt. This has happened on rare occasions. Since World War II, the federal government has only managed to run less than 10 such surpluses. President Harry Truman was the first to turn the government finances around after President Franklin Roosevelt's years of deficits. President Truman had surpluses in 1947, 1948, and 1951.

President Dwight Eisenhower also managed to run smaller surpluses in 1957 and 1958. There was not another government surplus for more than forty years until 1998 when President Bill Clinton signed a deal with Congress that achieved an $87.9 billion surplus. This surplus grew to $290 billion by 2000.

The last surplus came under President George W. Bush who had a $154 billion carryover surplus in 2001. On these rare occasions, the Federal government was able to pay down the federal debt temporarily. These surpluses were followed by half a trillion to trillion dollar deficits per year for most of the next decade.

Federal Reserve System

The Federal Reserve System is the United States' central banking system. It is made up of the Federal Open Market Committee, the Federal Reserve Board, 12 regional Federal Reserve Banks, and state and national member banks.

Seven members make up the Board of Governors. These the President appoints to 14 year terms upon approval by the Senate. The reason this system became established was to manage the movement of credit and money in the U.S. Congress set up this system in 1913. The U.S. had experienced a variety of central banks since 1791. The country needed a more stable banking system to help encourage a stronger economy.

Practically every bank in the U.S. participates in the Federal Reserve System. The program requires these institutions to keep a set amount of their assets deposited with their area Federal Reserve Bank. The Board of Governors determines how much these reserve requirements will be. The Board of Governors changes these required reserves in order to significantly influence the money supply that is circulating in the economy.

This Federal Reserve System provides a few different functions to the country. It is a bank for all the banks. A great number of interbank transactions go through this system. Banks may also borrow money from the Federal Reserve if they can not get credit from anywhere else. The system only gives them credit in emergencies or as it is unavailable on the open markets.

The Federal Reserve also functions like the bank of the government. The inbound and outbound payments of the tax system process via a checking account at the bank. The Fed further supplies the currency of the United States even though they do not produce it. They also purchase and sell government securities like Treasury Bills and Bonds.

Among the more important functions of this system is its purpose as a regulatory agency. They act as policeman to the banking sector to protect consumers' rights and to ensure smooth functions. They are also the main resource for banks and the public in times of financial crises or a panic surrounding the banks.

National banks have to be members of the system. In order to qualify, they are made to deposit the reserve requirements from their customer checking and savings accounts in their regional Federal Reserve bank. They must also keep mandatory reserve levels with this bank. Every nationally chartered bank has to be a member of the system. State chartered banks are also encouraged to join as members of the system.

The need for this Federal Reserve System became apparent after several failed attempts at establishing a uniform banking system in the United States. The first central bank was the First Bank that existed from 1791 to 1811. The Second Bank took over this role from 1816 to 1836. These two outfits proved to be the U.S. Treasury Department's only official representatives. This meant that they were the only organizations issuing and promoting the official U.S. currency.

Every other bank in the country ran under private auspices or as a state chartered organization. Each bank had its own bank notes which competed against the two U.S. banks as currency that could be redeemed for face value.

The first National Bank Act that Congress passed in 1863 allowed for a regimen of National Banks that would be supervised. Banks had to abide by certain operating practices, rules for making and issuing loans, and capital amount minimums kept in the banks. The Act effectively killed the non national individual bank currencies by creating a 10% tax on all state level banknotes.

Federal Trade Commission (FTC)

The FTC Federal Trade Commission proves to be the agency responsible for protecting the American consumers. They strive to stop tricky, fraudulent, and unfair practices in business in the nation's marketplaces. They also disburse valuable information to consumers that helps them to recognize, stop, and sidestep these frauds.

The FTC accepts consumer complaints by phone, email, their website, and through the mail. They take these complaints and enter them into a database that is called the Consumer Sentinel Network. This secure online tool is utilized for investigation purposes by literally hundreds of criminal and civil agencies for law enforcement throughout the United States and overseas.

What the FTC would like to do is to stop these types of deceptive and non-competitive business dealings before they hurt consumers. They are also attempting to improve consumer opportunities so that they are better informed about and comprehend the nature of competition. The agency attempts to perform all of these tasks without putting too many burdens and restrictions on businesses activities that are legitimate.

Congress created the FTC back in 1914. Originally its mandate lay in stopping unfair means of competition in trade and business caused by the trusts. They were a part of the government's stated goal to bust up these trusts. Congress has given them more authority to monitor and fight practices that were against fair competition over the years by passing other laws.

The government enacted another law in 1938 that was broadly addressed to stop any deceptive or unfair practices and acts. They have continued to receive direction and discretion to govern a number of other laws that protect consumers over the subsequent years. Among these are the Pay Per Call Rule, the Telemarketing Sales Rule, and the Equal Credit Opportunity Act. Congress passed another law in 1975 that gave the Federal Trade Commission the ability to come up with rules that regulated trade throughout the industries.

The FTC has a vision for the American economy. They want to see one that has healthy competition between producers. They also desire to see consumers able to obtain correct information. Ultimately the government agency looks for all of this to create low priced and superior quality goods. They encourage innovation, efficiency in business, and choice for consumers.

This agency carries out its vision with three strategic goals. It starts with them protecting consumers by heading off trickery and deception in the business and consumer marketplace. They desire to keep competition going strong. In this role, they stop mergers and business dealings that they believe are against competition. They also work to increase their own performance with consistently improving and excellent managerial, individual, and organizational efforts.

All of these goals and efforts combine to make the FTC one of the government agencies that most impacts each American citizen's economic and personal life. They are the only government entity that possesses a mandate for both competition jurisdiction and consumer protection in large segments of the U.S. economy. They go after aggressive and effectual enforcement of the laws.

The FTC shares its knowledge with international, state, and federal groups and agencies. The group creates research tools at a variety of conferences, workshops, and hearings every year. They also develop and distribute easy to understand educational materials for business and consumer needs in the transforming technological and global market.

The FTC carries out its work through its Bureaus of Economics, Competition, and Consumer Protection. They receive assistance from the Office of General Counsel. Seven regional offices around the country help them to carry out their mandate.

Five Year Plans

Five year plans are economic and social roadmaps that China began issuing in 1953. These were based upon the old Soviet central planning procedures. The Soviet Union collapsed in the early 1990s. Its plans are now a historical footnote. China continues to implement these plans every five years like a clock. They consistently show the world what China is attempting to focus on and accomplish. China has a history of meeting many if not most of its five year plan goals.

The government drafts and implements its plans on many levels. These include the district, local, provincial, and central government sectors. Industry regulators are also a part of the process. Most of these government divisions have their own five year plans as well. The NDRC National Development and Reform Commission draft the central government's plan. In these are detailed economic goals that include GDP growth rates.

Social development focuses on improvements in other important areas like education and healthcare. They come up with these specific targets after consulting with a variety of ministries and experts in industry and academia. Chinese regulators on all levels utilize these targets as they work through the implementing the period of the plan.

China spends years preparing these plans. They started talking about the goals of the 13th five year plan to run from 2016 to 2020 back in April of 2013. These plans set directions for the government priorities and policies. China met the majority of both economic and social goals they set out in the 12th FYP that concluded at the end of 2015.

These attained goals included average growth rates of seven percent, GDP services share at four percentage points higher, and seven percent annual increase to rural and urban incomes. Areas they struggled in were reducing carbon targets, raising non fossil fuels energy production, and increasing energy efficiency.

China relaxed its 35 year old one child policy as the biggest change in its current 13th FYP. This showed how the government is concerned about maintaining economic growth in the future as its population ages. For main economic targets, they set a GDP growth rate of average 6.5% per year. They also want to raise disposable income per capita by 6.5% each year. The leadership felt that this would make them into a “moderately prosperous society.”

The plan also continues on its path of reforms. Markets will have more influence and the state owned industries will be retooled. They will shift the economy to services from heavy industry. Services will represent a greater contributor towards GDP. The goal is for them to contribute 56% of the total GDP by 2020. China has also committed to lessen the state interventions into everything from account interest rates to gas prices.

They aim to increase the capacity of nuclear power to 58 gigawatts and the high speed rail network to 30,000 kilometers or 18,600 miles. The country is to build minimally 50 new airports for civilians. The government wants to develop a new 50 million urban area jobs. In support of this they want to see their urban residency rise to 60% of the whole population by the year 2020.

For other social changes China intends to significantly address the pollution problems of the past. They hope to limit energy consumption to less than five billion tons of coal equivalent. They also want to reduce their total energy consumption by 15 percent and cut carbon dioxide emissions by 18%. All of this working together is supposed to improve their sometimes horribly polluted air. The goal for city air quality is to see it rated at a minimally good rating for 80% of the time.

Foreign Exchange

Foreign exchange involves converting the currency of one nation into another nation's currency. Foreign exchange rates can be set in several different ways determined by the country's government. Free market economies allow their currency to float freely most of the time. The value of the money is determined by the markets according to supply and demand factors.

Other nations choose to peg the value of their money to a stronger and more stable currency like the U.S. dollar or the Euro. They might also choose to use a basket of currencies for such a peg. A third alternative is for a country's government to fix the value of their money at a set rate. The majority of nations choose to allow their foreign exchange rates to float freely versus the ones of other nations. This causes them to fluctuate up and down constantly throughout the day.

Sometimes nations which allow the value of their money to float freely will choose to intervene in foreign exchange markets to devalue their exchange rate. They might feel that their money's value has risen too fast and is hurting the competitiveness of their exports. As their exchange rate rises, the cost of their goods becomes more expensive to customers in foreign markets. In such a case, the country may announce that they are buying their own money at a lower rate or they may sell it off in Forex markets. Interventions like this tend to be less common except in volatile exchange environments.

Currency values are usually set by the forces of the market and are based on a number of national and international elements. These include trade and investment, flows of tourism, and geo political event risk. Trade and investment requires that the companies or nations purchase the host nation's money for the transaction. Investors may also want to purchase investments in another country. They would need that nation's money in order to make such investments.

When tourists come to visit a nation, they require the local money. They will exchange their own country's money for that of the one which they are visiting. Every one of these transactions constantly requires foreign exchange. This explains why the forex markets are the largest financial marketplaces in the world by far.

Banks handle this foreign exchange between each other on an international level. This creates a forex market that operates 24 hours per day and six days a week. The major centers of foreign exchange are disbursed around the world. These trades and transactions mostly occur in eight major forex centers. These are London, New York City, Tokyo, Singapore, Switzerland (Zurich and Geneva), Hong Kong, Sydney, and Paris. Each of the transactions comes under the regulation of the Bank of International Settlements.

Floating exchange rates are set by the supply and demand of all of these trades. More demand for a currency against a stable supply will increase the value of it against another. The rates are also impacted by numerous economic reports and geopolitical events. Some of the better known and followed ones are unemployment rates, interest rate levels and decisions, manufacturing data, gross domestic product changes, and inflation reports.

For countries that choose to go the route of pegged exchange, their governments must artificially set and maintain their exchange rates. These rates do not change up and down throughout the day. Instead the government will reset its value on reevaluation dates. Emerging market countries often find this a useful means of managing their foreign exchange rates in order to ensure that they are stable. They will be required to maintain large reserves of their pegged currency so that they can manage the inevitable supply and demand changes that affect their own foreign exchange.

Friedrich Hayek

Friedrich Hayek was a renowned Austrian economist born in Vienna in 1899. He earned significant fame for an impressive variety of contributions in such diverse fields as economics, psychology, and political philosophy. His economic ideas came from the Austrian School in economics. They focused on the fact that knowledge is limited in nature. Hayek became especially famous for defending free market capitalism. He is today still remembered as among the most effective critics of the socialist idea that was mostly consensus during his life time.

A man of many specialties, Friedrich Hayek has been called an ultimate Renaissance man for the twentieth century. His substantial and discipline changing contributions impacted economics, psychology, and political sciences. These fields often find an idea is surpassed by expansions on the creators' original theories. Yet with von Hayek, a number of his important contributions were so eye opening that many scholars still read them to this day over fifty years after he envisioned and wrote them down.

A significant number of graduate students in economics today read and study his articles which he wrote in the decades of the 30's and 40's. Even now many of the insights they still draw from his writings are ground breaking in their disciplines. Author Daniel Yergin has claimed that Hayek was the foremost economist of the second half of the 1900s in his book entitled *Commanding Heights*.

Friedrich Hayek turned out to be the most famous articulator and defender of the Austrian Economics school of thought. This is most ironic as he stands out as the only important recent member of this school that could call Austria his birthplace where he was raised. Following World War I, von Hayek earned twin doctorate degrees in political science and law from the University of Vienna. He then joined up with Ludwig von Mise in his private seminar with other young up and coming economists.

By 1927, von Hayek had taken on the director position at the newly established Austrian Institute for Business Cycle Research. He received an invitation from Lionel Robbins in the early 1930s and accepted a faculty position at the famed London School of Economics where he remained for 18 years, eventually earning British citizenship in 1938.

In this important time, Friedrich Hayek worked on Austrian theories of monetarism, capital, and business cycles. He believed in an important connection and relationship between the three topics. Von Hayek believed that the market happened spontaneously as an unplanned entity. Though no one designed it, it grew slowly but steadily because of human interaction. Despite this, the market did not function perfectly anywhere.

In 1974, Friedrich Hayek received the greatest honor of his life by co-wining the Nobel Prize in Economics. He and partner Gunnar Myrdal won this famous prize because of their “pioneering work in the theory of money and economic fluctuations and for their penetrating analysis of interdependence of economic, social, and institutional phenomena.”

Friedrich Hayek died on March 23 in 1992. Following his death, several of the universities at which he had taught over the years honored him with tributes, by naming halls and auditoriums after him. In a field where economic theories come and go all the time, his are still revered as especially insightful and diligently learned half a century after he created them.

Fractional Banking System

The fractional banking system is also known as the fractional reserve banking system. This system is the way that virtually all modern day banks around the world operate. In a fractional reserve banking system, banks actually only maintain a small amount of their deposited funds in reserve forms of cash and other easily liquid assets.

The rest of the deposits they loan out, even though all of their deposits are allowed to be withdrawn at the customers' demand. Fractional banking happens any time that banks loan out money that they bring in from deposits.

Fractional banking systems are ones where banks constantly expand the money supply beyond the levels at which they exist. Because of this, total money supplies are commonly a multiple bigger than simply the currency created by the nation's central bank. The multiple is also known as the money multiplier. Its amount is determined by a reserve requirement that the financial overseers set.

This fractional reserve system is managed ultimately by central banks and these reserve requirements that they enforce. On the one hand, it sets a limit on the quantity of money that is created by the commercial banks. The other purpose of it is to make certain that banks keep enough readily available cash in order to keep up with typical withdrawal demands of customers. Even though this is the case, there can be problems. Should many depositors at once attempt to take out their money, then a run on the bank might occur. If this happens on a large national or regional scale, the possibility of a banking systemic crisis emerges.

Central banks attempt to reduce these problems. They keep a close eye on commercial banks through regulations and oversight. Besides that, they promise to help out banks that fall into difficulties by acting as their ultimate lender of last resort. Finally, central banks instill confidence in the fractional reserve banking system by guaranteeing the deposits of the customers of the commercial banks.

A significant amount of criticism has been leveled against this fractional reserve banking system. Mainstream critics have complained that because money is only created as individuals borrow from the banking system, the system itself forces people to take on debt in order for money to actually be created. They say that this debases the currency. The biggest problem that they have with the commercial banking system growing the money supply is that it is literally creating money from nothing.

Other critics associate fractional banking with fiat currencies, or money that is only valuable because the governments say that they are. They decry these as negative aspects of current money systems. They dislike that fractional banking systems and fiat money together do not place any limits on how much a money supply can ultimately grow. This can lead to bubbles in both capital markets and assets, such as real estate, stock markets, and commodities. All of these can be victims of speculation, which is made easier by the creation of money through debt in the fractional reserve system.

Free Market

Free Market is the term that refers to a system of exchange and trading that takes place voluntarily in a given economic jurisdiction. These markets have the characteristics of decentralization and spontaneous arrangements whereby the people involved are able to make real economic choices with their money. No country in the world has a completely free market. The degree of its freedom depends heavily on the legal framework and political rules. In some nations where markets are centrally planned or at least tightly regulated by an oppressive government (such as in the pariah state of North Korea), the only free markets may be enormous black markets which the government can not or chooses not to control or shut down.

The phrase Free Market is often utilized in place of the French idea of laissez-faire forms of capitalism. This phrase translates to “hands off.” When the majority of individuals and investors refer to free markets, they are describing economies where competition is relatively unhindered and transactions are done on a generally private basis between willing sellers and buyers. A better definition would be a market in which economic activity is voluntarily and not coerced or heavily restricted by oppressive governmental authority.

With this more inclusive definition, both voluntary socialism and laissez-faire capitalism are real examples of the free markets. It does not matter that the socialism involves public ownership of the factors of production. So long as a central government is not restricting or impeding the free exchange of goods and economic activity, it is still Free Market capitalism. Coercion can be allowed in free markets in the cases of mutually agreed to terms as part of voluntarily signed contracts. This is how tort law and lawsuits operate under free market capitalism, though legal cases are certainly coercive obstructions to free economic activity.

It is the free market that makes it possible for goods from all across the globe to be made available to consumers in different countries. It similarly provides the greatest possible opportunities to entrepreneurs and business people. They put their personal capital at risk in order to meet the desires (both now and in the future) of the many global consumers as effectively and price-efficiently as they can. These free markets allow for savings and investment to produce capital goods while boosting the productivity of the workers (and hopefully their wages as well). It usually increases the standard of living of the employees as part of the process. Freely competing markets encourage and foster technological process and innovation which helps the inventors to satisfy the future desires of consumers across the world in creative and groundbreaking new ways.

Free markets allow for and cause the development of financial markets over time. Such markets provide for the finance and capital needs of those individuals and businesses which require greater capital resources for their business ventures than they can fund alone. While some businesses may save money through thriftiness, others actually deploy their savings in an effort to make money by expanding or incubating a new business. Securities can then be traded on secondary markets to encourage both activities.

As an example, individuals and investors who save are able to sink their resources into either the bonds or stocks of corporations. When they buy bonds, investors are providing their current savings to the businesses and entrepreneurs in exchange for the contractual agreement to repay these savings along with interest. When they purchase stocks, they are selling their savings in exchange for future claims on earnings not yet realized by the corporation.

There are many constraints that central governing authorities and regulating agencies impose on the free markets. These all come with either a verbal or implied threat of force if they are not heeded. Some of these constraints include taxation, licensing requirements, price and wage controls, quotas on exports or production, employee hiring regulations, sourcing of goods regulations, fixed exchange rates, and general regulations of many different kinds. When these restrictions become too repressive, voluntary exchange usually still occurs outside the government's knowledge in a black market. The problems with such markets is that oligopolies and monopolies often form in these underground free markets as competition is often ineffective and the prices are heavily impacted.

G20

The G20 is the combined organization of developed and important developing nations. These countries make up 85% of the global economy and include two thirds of all the people on earth. As the powerful driving engine of the global economy, this group has been recognized as centrally important in tackling issues of world importance.

The G20 is comprised of central bank governors and finance ministers of the European Union (represented by the President of the European Central Bank and the European Council President) and the United States, the United Kingdom, Turkey, South Africa, Saudi Arabia, Russia, Mexico, South Korea, Japan, Italy, Indonesia, India, Germany, France, China, Canada, Brazil, Australia, and Argentina. The G20 is headed by a president. This individual position rotates every year among the constituent member states.

These central bank governors and finance ministers meet two times per year. They generally coordinate their meetings with those of the World Bank, International Monetary Fund, and the G20 summits. At the November 15-16 2015 meeting held in Turkey, around 4,000 delegates and 3,000 representatives of the world media participated or attended.

The G20 group actually formed back in 1999. The idea was to provide a more important voice and forum for developing countries in arranging the world economy. These meetings began as only informal sit downs of central bankers and finance ministers. The world's first G20 summit occurred in the midst of the 2008 global financial crisis from November 16-17. They met in Washington, D.C. Until this first summit, most important global economic issues and plans were tackled by the G8 or G7.

These represent only the economically important developed nations. At this first summit, the emerging market leaders wanted the United States to better regulate its financial markets. The U.S. at first refused. These developing leaders also wished to see the debt rating companies like Standard & Poor's and the hedge funds better regulated. They believed standards should be strengthened in derivatives trading and global accounting. G20 members blamed poor standards and regulations for the financial crisis that led to the worldwide Great Recession.

The 2015 summit meeting happened on November 15-16, 2015 in Antalya, Turkey. This particular meeting concentrated on an appropriate response to the Paris terrorist attack. Member nations consented to accepting refugees from the war on ISIS while promising to improve their border monitoring against potential terrorist threats.

The United States conceded to sharing more of its intelligence information with both France and the other member states. The U.S. refused to dispatch ground troops to Syria, but did promise to support the coalition of anti ISIS Iraqi and Syrian forces. The group agreed on additional steps to restrict the important sources of financing for the Islamic State.

The 2014 summit annual meeting occurred from November 15-16, 2014 in Brisbane, Australia. This meeting concentrated efforts on condemning the Russian invasion of the Ukraine. The membership also unanimously agreed to strive together to boost the growth of the global Gross Domestic Product to 2.1% by the year 2018. This would provide another $2 trillion to economies of the world.

Both the European Union and The United States twisted arms of other member states to act on worsening climate change. This was not in the official meeting agenda. Leaders agreed to help out the fight against Ebola virus in West Africa. President Obama also met on the sidelines with the leaders of Australia and Japan regarding a peaceful settlement to maritime conflicts over territories in the South China Sea.

The 2016 G20 meeting is scheduled to be held from September 4-5, 2016 in Hangzhou, China. It will be the eleventh such summit of the G20.

G8 Summit

The G8 Summit is a yearly meeting of the leaders of the powerful economies of the world. The annual G8 president for the year hosts the meetings. Technically there is no political or legal authority for the summit, and its outcomes are not internationally binding. Yet when the major eight world leaders concur on an issue, this promises enough authority to change the direction of global economic policies and growth. The G8 is made up of the United States, Great Britain, Canada, Italy, Germany, France, Japan, and Russia.

The founding six nations of the group held their first summit in Rambouillet, France back in 1975. In attendance were the U.S., France, Britain, Germany, Italy, and Japan. Canada joined the group the following year to round out the G7. In 1997, the other members consented for Russia to join, bringing it up to its format of eight countries. The group once again devolved to the G7 when Russia invaded the Crimea in the Ukraine and was suspended indefinitely.

The remaining members all agreed on disallowing Russia as a form of sanctions against its aggressive behavior against its neighbor in annexing Ukrainian territory. The G8 Summit regularly invites other critical global leaders to attend. This includes representatives for China, India, Mexico, the European Union, and Brazil. Other crucial international organizations are regularly invited, such as the heads of the United Nations, the World Bank, and the International Monetary Fund.

The G8 Summit proved its power and efficacy every year in over 30 years of annual meetings. In 2008 a noticeable shifting of power happened. The G8 discussed inflation in food prices and other critical world issues while entirely missing the impending 2008 global financial crisis and Great Recession.

This G8 Summit in 2008 occurred in July at the same time as Freddie Mac and Fannie Mae were failing and the LIBOR rates were sky rocketing. The Fed had just met in its first emergency meeting in more than 30 years to discuss saving Bear Stearns. This signified that the old financial world order had ended as the G20 met and took up the most important issue facing the world and its economies.

Their summit tackled the economic and financial crisis at its roots. They asked the United States to better regulate its financial markets. The U.S. refused, instead permitting credit default swaps and other derivatives to be unregulated and blow up the world economy. This crisis made it clear that the emerging market economies were a critical part of any global solution. They had mostly sidestepped the financial crisis and clearly saw the flaws in the developed market economies and financial markets which had caused it. From this point forward, the G20 had the reputation of being the most crucial meeting in the world of all the important global leaders.

The 2015 G8 Summit (G7 Summit) was held on June 8, 2015 in Emau Castle in Germany. The G7 came out with a plan to phase out fossil fuels around the globe entirely by the year 2100. It did not sufficiently address either a cohesive plan to take down ISIS or the ongoing Greek debt crisis. Instead it left this last matter to the IMF and EU for resolution.

The 2014 Summit was originally intended to be held in Sochi, Russia and hosted by Russian President Vladimir Putin. The G7 cancelled this meeting and opted for an emergency summit on June 7-8, 2014 in Brussels, Belgium. They pledged $5 billion in economic aid to Ukraine and strengthened the economic sanctions against aggressive Russia. They also agreed to provide greater support to the efforts of the WHO to lessen such dangerous infectious diseases as Ebola and Tuberculosis.

The 2016 G7 summit happened from May 26-28, 2016 in Ise-Shima, Japan. As has become a recent tradition, Russia was not invited.

Gold Reserves

Gold Reserves are the amount of gold which nations and some international organizations hold to secure the value of their currency or to give credibility to their central bank policies. They are also utilized as a method of making international payments to other nations in order to settle outstanding bills and claims.

Such reserves (as a percentage of total reserves) that countries maintain were far larger from the 1700s through outbreak of World War I. This was because of the successful and stable policy of the gold standard that countries such as Great Britain and its empire pioneered throughout the globe.

For thousands of years, gold has been a means of exchange to one degree or another for empires, kingdoms, and nations around the world. During most of the time from the 1600s to 1900s, gold became even more critically important even after paper currency arose. This gold backed up the value of the paper money and could be exchanged for paper currency. Paper money served as legitimate claims on the gold reserves of the central banks of important nations for hundreds of years. International trade was settled in gold.

This helps to explain why countries had to build up and inventory a large supply of gold reserves. This was not only for economic reasons, but also for political ones. The larger a nation's reserves proved to be, the greater their economic strength was regarded. This was an internationally accepted standard at least until the beginning of the First World War. In those difficult years, many nations abandoned their gold standards because they could no longer afford to maintain them and simultaneously pay for the skyrocketing costs of the devastating global "Great War."

Nowadays no modern governments demand that all of their money be backed up by their gold reserves. Switzerland alone requires as much as 25 percent of their Swiss francs to be backed by equivalent gold holdings in their reserves. Despite this fact, most governments of the world still keep enormous quantities of the yellow metal as a protection against economic disaster, world financial crises, or the outbreak of hyperinflation. Most years, governments collectively boost their reserves by literally hundreds of tons. Canada is almost unique in that it has chosen to totally liquidate its reserves of the precious metal.

Gold remains the most widely watched and heavily traded world wide commodity, per a Futures magazine report in 2013. This is in part because non-government groups such as individuals, investors, and businesses recognize that gold is the ideal hedge against inflationary outbreaks or global and national recession. National gold reserves are always described in numbers of metric tons.

Though its stocks are no longer what they once were as a percentage of global gold holdings, the United States owns the biggest single stock pile of gold reserves on earth with a considerable lead on the second biggest holder. The U.S. holdings still amount to about the equivalent of the next three biggest national holders combined. The other countries in the top five nation holders are Germany, Italy, France, and China. The International Monetary Fund claims to have more gold holdings than Italy yet less than those Germany owns.

Per 2014, the national gold holdings were broken down accordingly. The United States owned 8,133.5 tons. Under the system of the Breton Woods international currency exchange mechanism, the U.S. stored somewhere between 90 percent and 95 percent of all global gold reserves in American-based vaults. Germany had 3,387.1 tons in 2014. Italy maintained 2,451.8 tons. France owned 2,435.4 tons. China held 1,054.1 tons officially, though the majority of analysts concur that the Chinese massively under-report their true gold holdings. This is likely to be the case as China is the world's largest gold miner. It allows them to add gold quietly to their reserves without having to make purchases on the international gold markets.

Gold Standard

The gold standard represents a centuries' used system of money for backing up currencies with tangible, physical gold holdings in a central bank vault. Under the gold standard, the basic economic currency unit proved to be a pre set amount of gold by weight. Several different types of gold standards exist.

The Gold specie standard proves to be a system where the money unit itself is represented by gold coins that are in circulation. Alternatively, it could be represented by an exchange unit of value that is literally expressed in units against a specific gold coin that circulates, along with other coins that are minted from a metal with less value, such as silver or copper.

Conversely, the gold exchange standard usually has to do with silver and other valuable metal coins that are circulating. In this type of exchange system, the monetary authorities promise that a set exchange rate against the currency of another country practicing the gold standard will be maintained. This gives rise to a gold standard that is not literal but still de facto. The silver coins circulating then trade with a set external value in gold terms that stands independently of the actual silver value contained within the coins.

The most common gold standard that has been seen in the last few hundred years turns out to be the gold bullion standard. The gold bullion standard refers to a money system where no gold coins are actually circulating throughout the economy. Instead, the monetary authorities have consented to exchange a set amount of gold in exchange for their paper currency. This is done at a set price that is established for the paper currency that circulates.

The gold bullion standard existed in the world economy from the 1700's until 1971. During this span of almost three hundred years, the values of major world currencies proved to be exceptionally stable, as were the supplies of money in existence. This resulted from a restriction of the gold standard that only allowed such paper currency to be printed as greater amounts of gold existed in the respective nation's treasury and vaults. The positive of this proved to be that the world could count on currencies that did not fluctuate wildly in value or decline consistently over time. Governments disliked the gold standard as it kept them from increasing the money supply or spending more money than the country actually had. They found it too restrictive.

The gold standard in the world collapsed when President Nixon initiated what became known as the Nixon shock by unilaterally taking the country off of gold exchange and convertibility for dollars in 1971. The currency of both the U.S. and most countries of the world then became Fiat currencies, only backed up by the government decree. Since the gold standard was abandoned, the U.S. dollar has declined so severely that a single dollar in 1971 would today be worth $35 2010 dollars.

Grexit

Grexit is the clever abbreviation for the idea of a Greek exit from the Eurozone. The feared event of Greece returning to its old currency until 2001 the Drachma never occurred thanks to a variety of bailouts in exchange for austerity measures. This did not stop it from threatening to collapse several European banks which held Greek debt and infecting the sovereign bonds of other similarly afflicted countries like Spain and Portugal.

The global financial crisis pushed over Greece's precarious financial position. In 2009 in only the first quarter, the country's GDP plunged by 4.7%. At the same time its deficit skyrocketed to more than 12% of the national GDP. Credit downgrades were not long in following. All three of the major agencies Moody's, Standard and Poor's, and Fitch began downgrading Greek debt until S&P finally cut it to junk level in 2010. The resulting yields on 10 year Greek bonds rose to over 44% at their worst point in March of 2012.

The socialist government began a series of cuts to attempt to stabilize its shrinking finances. In the initial austerity measures the socialist party passed in 2009 they cut the spending and government jobs wages by 10% and raised the age for retirement. During the next three years, they passed other austerity packages that severely cut back pay for government jobs, laid off public workers, increased taxes, cut minimum wages, cut pensions, slashed defense and health spending, and loosened the procedures for laying off employees.

Not all of these measures were evenly implemented. Interest groups with powerful allies were able to stall the ones that impacted them while those impacting the poor and middle classes moved forward. Unemployment soared from slightly more than 10% to around 28% by September of 2013. More than 40% of Greek children live in poverty. Nearly 50% of ages 15 to 24 year old Greeks are unemployed.

In order to qualify for international help from the IMF and EU, Greece was told to cut its expenditures still further. They were forced to begin a series of humiliating austerity measures and to enact painful structural reforms in order to receive the bailout money that was needed to stave off financial collapse.

Prime Minister Papandreou asked for a bailout from the IMF and EU in April of 2010. These groups responded to the calls for help by approving a 110 billion over three years ($147 billion when offered) bailout. This represented the largest bailout of a sovereign nation in history. In order to receive it, Greece had to go through yet another series of agonizing austerity measures.

Greece needed still more help and in February of 2012 received approval for a second package of bailout money. The EU nations, the European Central Bank, and the IMF known collectively as the Troika increased their money to Greece by another $172 billion bringing them to a total of 246 billion worth $319 billion in those days. Greece was required to lower its debt down from the 160% GDP at the time to 120% by 2020. Greek bond holding banks took a 53.5% haircut on their bonds' face value. This amounted to as much as 75% loss of the real value of the debt.

Regular Greeks felt betrayed by their own leadership and the leaders of fellow Eurozone countries such as Chancellor Angela Merkel of Germany. Their economy continued to slide in and out of recessions. Greece finally reached the point of a referendum on the policies and austerity that had brought the country to this low point.

More than 60% of Greeks who voted rejected austerity in the results. This led to fears that Greece would drop out of the Euro if the demands of Syriza party leader and Prime Minister Alexis Tsipras for a better bailout package were not met. This departure from the Eurozone never materialized, as Greece continued to receive periodic monetary help and support from the Troika every quarter. Greeks never saw most of this $320 billion in bailout money, as it instead generally passed through the country on its way to repay holders of Greek debt.

Gross Domestic Product (GDP)

GDP stands for the entire value in dollars of all goods and services that have actually been produced within the nation in a particular period of time, commonly a year. A simpler way of putting GDP is how large the economy proves to be.

The Gross Domestic Product turns out to be among the most closely watched and important measurements for how healthy the economy is. GDP is commonly given out as a comparison against a prior year or quarter. When the financial news reports that the Gross Domestic Product has increased by three percent year on year, it is referring to the economy having expanded by three percent during the last year.

Coming up with the actual measurement of Gross Domestic Product is complex. In simplest terms, it is figured up in one of two methods. The income approach works by totaling up the earnings of all individuals in the country over a year. The expenditure approach simply tallies up the money that everyone in the nation spends over the year. It stands to reason that through both means you should come to approximately a similar total.

With the income approach, economists take all of the employees' compensation in the nation. They add this to all of the profits that both non incorporated, as well as incorporated, companies have made throughout the country. Finally they add on all taxes paid minus subsidies given. This is known as the GDP(I) method of calculation. The expenditure based means proves to be the more typically utilized method. To figure up GDP this way, all government spending, net exports, consumption, and investment in the country have to be tallied up together.

You can not overstate the importance of GDP to an economy's growth and production. Almost every person within the nation is massively impacted by gross domestic product. If an economy is in good shape, then wages will rise and unemployment will prove to be low as businesses require greater quantities of labor in order to produce to keep up with the expanding economy. Major changes to Gross Domestic Product, revised to the downside or upside , have significant repercussions for the stock markets. The reasons for this are simple to grasp.

Economies that are contracting translate to smaller amounts of profits for corporations. This leads to lower prices for stocks. Investors also become nervous about decreasing growth in GDP, since it commonly means that the nation's economy is falling into recession or is already in a recession.

Conversely, economies that are expanding signify that corporations' profits in general will be higher. Investors bid stock prices up on this news as they become increasingly confident in the future economic prospects. Because of these effects of Gross Domestic Product on peoples' lives, it could be said to be the most significant economic measurement for all of the people in the country in general.

Hyperinflation

In the field of economics, hyperinflation proves to be inflation, or rising prices over time, that is extremely high and even beyond controlling. This state of the economy exists as the overall levels of pricing in a certain country are rising sharply and quickly at the same time as the actual values of these economic goods remain roughly the same price as measured in other more stable currencies. In other words, the nation's own currency is diminishing in value rapidly, commonly at rate that grows in pace.

The IASB, or International Accounting Standards Board, gives a precise definition of hyperinflation. They state that when the rate of inflation during three cumulative years nears one hundred percent total, or at least twenty-six percent each year compounded annually for three consecutive years, then hyperinflation has been reached. Other economists such as Cagan have declared hyperinflation to be when inflation is greater than fifty percent each month. Hyperinflation can witness the overall price levels go up by five to ten percent and higher even in single days for extended periods of time. This stands in sharp contrast to regular inflation which is commonly only reported over a quarterly or annual basis.

As greater and greater amounts of inflation are created in each printing of money instance, a truly vicious cycle takes effect. Such hyperinflation is clearly evident as the money supply grows at an uninterrupted rate. It is typically seen alongside the population's unwillingness to keep the hyper-inflationary currency for any longer than they have to in order to use it for any hard good that will prevent them from losing more actual purchasing power. Hyperinflation is typically a part of wars and their after effects, social or political upheavals, and currency meltdowns such as seen in Zimbabwe.

Hyperinflation is a phenomenon that is unique to fiat currencies that are not backed up by anything but a government's faith and trust. As the money supply is not limited by normal restraints like gold in a vault, it is instead run by a paper money standard. The supply of it is completely dependent on the discretion of the government.

Hyperinflation commonly leads to intense and long lasting economic depressions. This is not always the case though. In Brazil which suffered in the grips of hyperinflation for thirty years in the 1964 to 1994 period, the government managed to avoid economic collapse by valuing all non-monetary goods, services, and investments for the whole economy in an involved index. The government supplied this daily updated index that they measured with the daily Brazilian currency against the United States dollar.

In contrast to Brazil, Zimbabwe did not bother to set up such an index measured against the dollar. They did offer the day by day changes in the U.S. dollar as a comparison for everyone in the country to see. This voluntary comparison only served to worsen the problem and finally destroyed the real value of non monetary items that did not get updated as expressed against the Zimbabwe dollar. All monetary items in the country finally lost every bit of value during the hyper-inflationary meltdown.

Income Distribution

Income distribution proves to be the way that a country's entire gross domestic product is actually shared out among all members of the population. This has long been a main concern of the study of economics and related governmental economic policies. The classical economists of the discipline such as Adam Smith, David Ricardo, and Thomas Malthus were principally concerned about the factor of income distribution. This refers to the actual distribution of income as it pertains to the principal factors of production, such as capital, labor, and land.

More modern day economists have similarly turned their attentions to the topic in recent decades. They have been mostly preoccupied with the income distribution as it pertains to both households and individual consumers in economies. There are many public policy issues which involve such relationships as those of economic growth and income inequality. These have led to the creation of various measurements to analyze income distribution in a society and economy. Chief among these is the Lorenz Curve representation. It is correlated closely with such income inequality measurements as the highly respected and internationally utilized Gini coefficient.

There are many different related causes of and factors leading to income inequality in the world today. Some of the more important ones prove to be tax and other economic policies, fiscal policies, monetary policies by central banks such as the Federal Reserve and Bank of England, labor union policies, the labor market in given industries and regions, individual skills sets of specific workers, impacts of automation and technology, the negative effects of globalization, educational levels of workers in different regions and countries, race, gender, and culture.

Thanks to such useful concepts as the pervasive Gini coefficients, a few well respected organizations including especially the United States' Central Intelligence Agency and the international body the United Nations have been able to measure actual levels of income inequality on a country to country comparison basis.

The World Bank similarly employs the Gini coefficient index as it has consistently proven to be a dependable and accurate index measurement for comparing and contrasting income distribution on a nation by nation basis. This widespread index runs a measurement gamut of from 0 to 1. On this scale, 0 represents complete equality, while 1 depicts total inequality in the society or economy in question. As of the year 2016, the world's Gini index measures fittingly at 0.52.

Income inequality may be looked at through two different statistical approaches. These are intra country inequality that looks at the conditions within the nation itself. The other is inter country inequality that amounts to the various inequality levels between one country and the next one.

A May of 2011 report that the OECD researched and published demonstrated a disturbing trend regarding income inequality and income distribution among the OECD developed nations. The income gap between poor and rich in these developed nations, practically all of which represent the high income economies, "has reached its highest level for over 30 years, and governments must act quickly to tackle inequality."

The United States is a classic example of this troubling point. Income in America has become so unevenly distributed throughout the prior 30 years that the earners of the top quintile 20 percent now earn a greater share than the combined four quintiles or bottom 80 percent together do. This is the kind of dangerous and damaging statistic upon which violent class based revolutions are built.

Inflation

Inflation proves to be prices rising over time. It is specifically measured as the increase in a given basket of goods and services' prices. These goods and services are taken to represent the entire economy. Inflation is also the going up in cost of the average prices of goods and services as measured by the CPI, or consumer price index. The opposite of inflation is known as deflation. Deflation turns out to be the falling of an average level of prices. The point that separates the two from each other, both deflation and inflation, is price stability, or no change in the costs of goods and services.

Inflation has almost everything to do with the amount of money available. It is inextricably tied to the money supply. This gives rise to the popularly remarked observation that inflation is actually an excessive number of dollars chasing too small a quantity of goods. Comprehending the way that this works is easier when considering an example.

Pretend for a moment that the world possessed only two commodities: oranges that are gathered up from orange trees and paper money created by government. In seasons where rain is limited and the oranges are few as a result, the cost of oranges should go up. This is because the same number of printed dollars would be competing for a smaller number of oranges.

On the other hand, if a bumper crop of oranges are seen, then the cost of oranges should drop, since the sellers of oranges have no choice but to cut prices to sell off their large inventory of oranges. These two examples illustrate inflation in the former and deflation in the latter. The main difference between the real world and this example is that inflation measures changes in the price movement on average of many or all goods and services, and not simply one.

The quantity of money in an economy similarly impacts the amount of inflation present at any given time. Should the government in the example above choose to print enormous amounts of money, then there will be many dollars for a relatively constant number of oranges, as in the lack of rain scenario. So inflation is created by the number of dollars going up against the quantities of oranges that exist, or overall goods and services existing. Deflation, as the opposite of inflation, would be the numbers of dollars dropping compared to the quantity of oranges available.

Because of this, levels of inflation result from four different factors that often work together in combination. The demand for money could drop. The supply of money could expand. The available supply of various other goods might decline. Finally, the demand for other goods increases.

Even though these four factors do work in correlation, economists say that inflation is mostly a currency driven event. This means that in the vast majority of cases, it results from governments tampering with the money supply. Generally, they do this by over printing their own currency to have money to pay for spending, resulting in higher inflation.

Inflationary Bias

Inflationary Bias refers to the opposite of deflationary bias. Both of these are government monetary and/or fiscal policy prejudices. Governments are forced to take one of two positions with reference to their monetary policy and interventions in an economy. Inflationary bias turns out to be the one which the vast majority of central banks and sovereign nation policy makers pursue for several important reasons.

Such an Inflationary Bias results from discretionary policies of national governments. If they are utilized properly with regards to the labor market, these biases cause a higher than ideal inflation level without leading to any transitions in income increases. At the same time, this bias results from the goals of those nations which are saddled with public debt levels. They would pursue these policies with a goal of fostering inflation over the medium to longer term.

There are economic theories that persuasively argue governments have a natural affinity for and tendency towards Inflationary Bias policies. The Barro-Gordon model demonstrates that the government's ability to manipulate the economy will cause it to skew towards a bias that is inflationary by nature. According to such a model, countries will try to maintain the country's national unemployment rates at lower than the naturally occurring levels. This causes a wage and price inflation that is higher than their normally occurring level. In the end, this will lead to an aggregate inflationary level that proves to be greater than the normal level of inflation.

The economic theories that are more traditional also suggest that this Inflationary Bias will be present any time that fiscal and monetary policies become enacted at the discretion of the policy makers and central bankers instead of being rules based. Still other economists argue that this bias will even be present if the policy makers are not bent on reducing unemployment to lower than normal levels and even if the policies operate off of rules instead.

As there are so many perils from such Inflationary Biases, economists have suggested a variety of measures to stop it from occurring. Some of them have argued for appointing only conservatively ideological central bankers.

According to these arguments, the countries ought to set out aimed for inflationary targets and goals. When these rates of inflation are surpassed by real economic data releases, there could be a punishment of some type given out to the central bankers.

In truth and point of fact, the majority of important countries now do state their optimal inflation rate targets in their policy setting meetings, press conferences, and notes from closed door meetings alike. For most Western nation policy makers and central banks like the United States Federal Reserve, Great Britain's Bank of England, the Euro Zone's European Central Bank, and the Japanese Central Bank, this level amounts to a desired two percent inflation target over the medium to long term time frame.

For those nations that opt to go with the opposite of an inflationary bias, the only other choice is the deflationary bias. The problem with deflationary biases is that they only work for countries, businesses, and consumers which are not saddled down with enormous debt levels. This is because a deflationary bias will cause debts to progressively cost more in real terms over time even as they reward savers and creditors. Governments are especially afraid of this policy bias as they are mostly running budgetary deficits year in and year out. Only a handful of countries run government budget surpluses in point of fact.

Interbank Market

The Interbank Market refers to the modern day financial system which involves banks trading cash and other instruments with other financial institutions and banks. This never involves banks trading money with non-financial businesses, consumers, or retail investors. It is possible for interbank trading to be pursued by banks for the benefit of their bigger customers, yet in general such trading between banks proves to be proprietary. This means that it happens between banks on the behalf of their own company accounts.

Interbank markets also involve FOREX foreign exchange services in a commercial capacity of buying and selling currency pair investments. There can be long-term trading as well as huge quantities of shorter term, speculative nature currency trading. The Bank of International Settlements stated in information which they compiled and analyzed in 2004 that around fifty percent of all transactions on the world FOREX markets are strictly interbank market trade.

It was after the failure of the Bretton Woods agreement and the catastrophic decision of then-American President Richard Nixon to abandon the gold standard back in 1971 that the present-day form of the interbank market arose and developed. Currency exchange rates for the majority of the big and economically important industrial countries became freely floating at this time. It was only on occasion that the various national governments chose to intervene in the interbank markets where their own currencies were concerned.

These markets do not have any central or single location or authority. Instead, the trading occurs all over the world in every time zone and during six days per week from Sunday afternoon through Friday afternoon. The only exceptions to this schedule are the few internationally and unanimously recognized holidays, such as New Year's Day.

The arrival of this new floating rate system of exchange happened to occur as the inexpensive computer systems and program revolution emerged. This happy coincidence permitted for quickly executed, globally-based exchange trading for the first time in history. At first, voice brokers utilized the phone and later fax machines to match up sellers and buyers in these earliest days of the interbank FOREX trading. These eventually became replaced by the new fast and far more cost-effective computer systems.

The computer systems which became connected by the Internet in time could scan huge volumes of traders and obtain the most optimal price in this way. Thanks to both Bloomberg and Reuters who created impressive trading systems which became ubiquitous around the world, banks gained the ability to trade literally billions of dollars in transactions at the same time. On the busiest days in the FOREX and interbank markets nowadays, daily trading volume exceeds more than $6 trillion.

The biggest market participants are the interbank market makers. Such financial institutions have to be both willing and able to extend pricing to other players in the market besides requesting prices for themselves and their own interest in trades. Interbank market deals have minimums which start at $5 million. The majority of transactions are vastly larger. Sometimes they exceed a full billion dollars in only a single transaction. The biggest players in the interbank markets by far are United States market makers JP Morgan Chase Bank and Citicorp, German and European market maker Deutsche Bank, and Asian market maker (London- based) HSBC.

The majority of such spot transactions agreed on the interbank markets will settle two business days following the trade execution. The biggest exception to this policy lies with the American dollar versus the Canadian dollar. It settles the following day. This settlement delay requires banks to maintain extensive credit lines (even when these are current spot trades) with their peer financial institutions so that they can trade continuously.

To lower the risks inherent with settlement, most banks engage in netting agreements. These agreements require that an offsetting transaction must be done within the identical currency pair which will settle on the exact same day as the opposing transaction. In such a way, the banks are able to drastically reduce the quantity of money which must change hands, as well as the default risks which could happen if one trading bank suddenly and unexpectedly encountered financial problems.

International Financial Institutions (IFI)

International financial institutions (IFIs) are international financial organizations which multiple nations founded. They are subject to international law instead of the laws of any one single country. The IFIs are usually owned by national governments of the founding members.

Sometimes other international institutions or organizations are stakeholders as well. Even though there are IFIs that two or three nations created, the best known ones were developed by numerous national participants. The most famous international financial institutions arose following the Second World War in order to help rebuild Europe, as well as to offer the means of multinational cooperation in overseeing the world's financial system.

The largest international financial institution in the world today proves to be the European Investment Bank. In 2013, this organization possessed a balance sheet that amounted to 512 billion euros. This compares to the main component parts of the World Bank, the IBRD with $358 billion in assets as of 2014 and the IDA with its $183 billion in assets as of 2014. By means of comparison, the world's biggest international commercial banks boast assets each totaling between $2 - $3 billion, as with Britain's HSBC and the United States' JP Morgan Chase Bank.

Arguably the most important international financial institutions in the world today remain the ones which the Bretton Woods agreement founded in 1944. These are the World Bank and the International Monetary Fund. Both are participating members of the United Nations system. Their goals are to improve the standards of living in their respective member nations.

Each of these two organizations has its own approach to achieving this mandate, yet they complement each other. The IMF concentrates its efforts on larger macroeconomic issues. The World Bank instead focuses on developing the economies and reducing the poverty of member states over the longer term.

The World Bank and IMF came into being in July of 1944 at the internationally attended Bretton Woods Conference held in New Hampshire. The conference had a goal to build up a new framework of development and economic cooperation which would help to establish a more prosperous and stable global economy. Over 70 years later, this goal is still critical to the operations of both international financial institutions. Only the means they use to reach the goals has changed as different economic challenges and developments arise.

The World Bank mandate is to encourage poverty reduction and economic improvement longer term. They do this by offering financial and technical assistance to aid countries which are trying to reform sections of their economies or to develop particular projects. These projects could be delivering electricity and water, constructing health centers and schools, safeguarding the environment, or fighting disease. Such help as the World Bank provides is typically longer term in nature and funded by contributions from member nations as well as by issuing bonds. The staff of the World Bank is typically specialized in certain sectors, issues, or methods.

The IMF on the other hand operates under a mandate to foster monetary cooperation on an international level while it offers technical assistance and policy advice to help countries to develop and keep more prosperous and stronger economies. As part of this, the IMF offers loans. They also help nations to create policies and programs that will address their imbalance of payments if they are unable to obtain affordable term financing to meet their international financial obligations. These loans are either medium or short term. The funds come from the quota contributions' pool provided by member states. The staff of the IMF is mainly economists who possess vast experience with financial and macroeconomic issues.

International Monetary Fund (IMF)

The International Monetary Fund represents an international organization with membership of 189 different countries. As such it counts nearly all countries of the world among its almost global membership. This IMF seeks to achieve financial stability, helps to encourage worldwide monetary cooperation, pushes for economic growth that is sustainable and for high unemployment, helps to facilitate international trade, and attempts to lessen poverty throughout the world.

Members of the United Nations created the International Monetary Fund back in 1945 as a result of the idea initially conceived of at the important Bretton Woods UN conference held in New Jersey in the United States in July of 1944. Originally 44 nations attended this conference and looked for ways to rebuild the global economy. They wanted to create a way of fostering economic cooperation. The group collectively hoped to not repeat the mistakes of the 1930s. A currency devaluing race to the bottom had led to the Great Depression in those years.

There were a number of original goals for the IMF. The organization was to encourage stability of exchange rates and monetary cooperation on an international scale. They were to promote and aid in the growth of a balanced international trade. IMF also had to help build up a system for balance of payments that was multilateral in scope. They also were designed to provide emergency resources to member states that suffered from problems with their balance of payments. Safeguards on the resources loaned out would b required.

With the early 1970's dissolution of the fixed exchange rates based on the gold standard set up at the Bretton Woods conference, their role changed some. They were no longer responsible for stable exchange rates and a balance of payments system based on pegged exchange rates. They became more of an organization that helps out member states in emergency economic need.

Today the IMF counts among its largest emergency borrowers Greece, Portugal, Ukraine, and Ireland. It also issues precautionary loans to members who may need to borrow based on particular conditions within their countries. The countries with the largest precautionary loan amounts agreed on include Poland, Mexico, Colombia, and Morocco. Between the two groups, the IMF has committed itself to $163 billion. Of this amount $137 billion has not yet been drawn.

The International Monetary Fund still works to safeguard the global monetary system. They watch over the system of international payments and free floating exchange rates so that nations and their populations can engage in transactions with each other. In 2012, the fund received an expanded mandate in part as a result of the chaos in the Great Recession. This bigger mandate includes all issues pertaining to the financial sectors and all macroeconomic issues that have to do with global stability.

The International Monetary Fund has its headquarters in Washington, D.C. Their governance is by an executive board. The board is made up of 24 directors. Each of these directors represents either a group of nations or a single nation. The IMF maintains a global staff of 2,600 individuals who hail from 147 different countries.

The majority of the IMF's money comes from its quota system. Every member is given a quota that they must contribute. This amount is based on the nation's economic size in the global economy. The member state's maximum contributions are limited to this quota. When countries join, they pay as much as one-quarter of their quota in a widely traded foreign currency like the pound, euro, dollar, or yen or as SDR Special Drawing Rights made up of a basket of these currencies. The other three-quarters they pay from their own currency.

International Monetary Unit

International Monetary Unit can refer to two different things. It could be the U.S. dollar, which is the world's primary reserve currency. The International Monetary Unit is also the Special Drawing Rights, which are the currency units that the International Monetary Fund issues.

Special drawing rights are not an actual unique currency per se. They are units that are made up of a special basket of currencies. These days, these are comprised of U.S. Dollars, British Pounds, Japanese Yen, and Euros. The Special Drawing Rights, also known as SDR's, can be said to be International Monetary Units since they prove to be reserve assets for international foreign exchange. The International Monetary Fund actually allocates them to different countries. These SDR's offer the ability to get foreign currencies when a country needs hard cash for emergencies and other financial crises.

Although they are still expressed in units against U.S. dollars, the Special Drawing Rights remain the International Monetary Fund's only unit of account. They have their own currency code, XDR. They may be only little used now for an International Monetary Unit, but their utilization is growing, particularly at the insistence of Russia, China, and the United Nations.

Since the end of the Second World War, the U.S. dollar has proven to be the world's main reserve asset for foreign exchange. This makes it a primary candidate for the world's International Monetary Unit. As over sixty percent of central bank reserves are still held in dollars, it is unarguably the world's reserve currency even though many nations would like to see this changed and its share of reserves has been dropping consistently for some time now. Countries ranging from China and Russia, to Iran and Venezuela, to France have all called for a new International Monetary Unit to be established, particularly in the wake of the Financial Crisis of 2007 to 2010.

A new international monetary unit may arise to replace the dollar, but it does not look to happen any time too soon. This is mainly because no suitable replacement for it has been found yet. Euros are not yet widely enough held, though they are gaining in share of reserves each and every year. Neither Japanese Yen, nor British Pounds, nor Swiss Francs are significantly representative enough of economic spheres of influence to be a viable challenger. The special drawing rights are one possible replacement for the dollar, as would be a gold backed International Monetary Unit. Gold served this purposes for several hundred years during the gold standard era of the 1700's to 1971.

Gold is a last candidate for a new International Monetary Unit. As it has universal appeal and acceptance, it does offer a strong challenge to the dollar. Gold is a hard international monetary unit to argue with because it does not bear the liabilities of any single nation. It can not be manipulated by any single government or corporation. This makes it a likely choice as at least part of a new International Monetary Unit in the coming century, if not the sole one.

Initiative for Policy Dialogue (IPD)

The Initiative for Policy Dialogue, also known as IPD, is a Columbia University based American non-profit organization of global economic reach and importance. Joseph E. Stieglitz the famous Nobel winning laureate in economics founded the group back in July of 2000. In this endeavor he had the financial support of such important heavyweight groups as foundations and governments. These included the Rockefeller, Ford, Mott, and McArthur Foundations as well as the governments of both Sweden and Canada.

This Initiative for Policy Dialogue proves to be an international network of over 250 world renowned economists, civil society representatives, political scientists, and active practitioners of various backgrounds from around the whole world. Their backgrounds are diverse and well represented of various inter-disciplines. The IPD uses this wide range of skills and tremendous resources in order to assist nations with effective solutions for urgent challenges, issues, and problems. They are also interested in building up the developing national institutions as well as civil societies.

It is the mission of the Initiative for Policy Dialogue to carry the pressing areas of concern from the developing world to both academics and American and other developed nations' policymakers and governments. Joseph Stieglitz the driving force behind this organization is well-placed and -suited to do this with his connections to governments and academia around the world. He serves as co-President of the organization.

As the Columbia University ranking "University Professor" in Economics at their business school, he is also involved with their School of International and Public Affairs. Stieglitz also serves as their Committee on Global Thought Chairman. He has chaired the United Nations Commission known as the "Experts on Reforms of the International Monetary and Financial System."

The U.N. established this committee after the devastating Great Recession, financial collapse, and economic crisis of 2007-2009 under the auspices of the President of the General Assembly. He has also served as the World Bank's Senior Vice President and Chief Economist, as well as President Clinton's Chairman of the Council of Economic Advisors. Stieglitz earned the Nobel Memorial Prize in Economics back in 2001. It is hard to find a more impressive resume in the world of economics. He was named among the top four most influential economists in the world.

The other co-President of the Initiative for Policy Dialogue is José Antonio Ocampo. Ocampo also works as Professor for the Columbia University School of International and Public Affairs. He is similarly a Member of the Columbia University Committee on Global Thought. Ocampo is internationally known for his role as the Chairman of the U.N. Committee for Development Policy. He has also served as Under Secretary-General at the United Nation's ECLAC Economic Commission for Latin America and the Caribbean. Previously he held the post of Colombia's Minister of Finance, Planning, and Agriculture.

The Initiative for Policy Dialogue has four main programs that help them to impact public policy and shape the world. Their Task Forces help experts from around the world to collaborate in order to investigate complicated issues of development so that they can offer alternative policies to governments. Their Country Dialogues work to better the quality of decisions which policy makers engage in regarding issues covering economics.

Their Journalism Program is the outlet which they use to improve the economic literacy of journalists so that they are able to more effectively report on the complex economic topics that affect developing nations. The Educational Programs attempt to explain the various issues combating both local and global decision making in the developing nations of the world.

John Maynard Keynes

John Maynard Keynes proved to be the English economist, professor, and journalist who also served in British government as a key economic advisor at the powerful British Treasury department. He has become best remembered for his at-the-time influential Keynesian economics. These theories had to do with the reasons for and solutions to long term unemployment.

Keynes was born to a middle class family of moderately successful prosperity on June 5th of 1883 in the famed university town of Cambridge, England. The man is best known for his economic theories that are still called after his name as "Keynesian economics." He wrote a critically important work entitled, The General Theory of Employment, Interest and Money from 1935-1936. This treatise argued that government-pushed policies of full employment could cure economic recessions. It has been called among the most influential books in all human history.

John Maynard Keynes had an academic for a father that helped to propel his lifelong passion for learning, teaching, research, and public service. John Neville Keynes his father served as economist and eventually academic administrator at the world-renowned King's College of Cambridge University. Even his mother could claim to be among the very first women graduates from Cambridge. Keynes attended the historic and prestigious university himself beginning in 1902. While studying there, Keynes came under the influence of economist Alfred Marshall. Marshall had such an impact on John that he switched from the classics and math studies to economics and politics.

In the 1920s, Keynes began to write pieces which were increasingly skeptical of the then-dominant laissez-faire style of economics that was very gently overseen by minor public policies. He stood against Britain returning back to the gold standard at a fixed rate in 1925 and demonstrated his concern about the long-term unemployment problems experienced by British textile workers, shipyard employees, and coal miners even before the Great Depression erupted.

Once Keynes wrote his internationally accepted greatest work The General Theory of Employment, Interest and Money, he became the most influential economist of his time. In this magnum opus, he argued for an economic solution utilizing programs of government-sponsored or -provided jobs to solve the persistent and sky-high unemployment. Some critics have argued that his book was unclear enough that no one is actually sure what Keynes was really trying to say. His arguments seemed to be that reducing the rates of wages would not help governments to lower unemployment. Instead, it would take government spending increases to lower unemployment. This would lead to a budget deficit, which he claimed would be a necessary evil in order to solve these terrible economic and social problems of the time. World governments were eager to find reasons to boost their spending. This explains why they adopted all of his principal views with enthusiasm. The majority of his academic peers also ascribed to his ideas in the 1930s and 1940s.

Yet weaknesses in Keynes theories would emerge as reality challenged it repeatedly. He himself argued that his policies would only work optimally in a society that was totalitarian. From the later 1940s through the later 1980s his economic model remained a central tenet of economics and such textbooks. Yet economists finally began to move away from unemployment problem fixation and on to economic growth issues. As they learned more about the links between inflation and unemployment, his once-widely touted model lost its importance.

John Maynard Keynes is well-remembered for two major services to Great Britain and the world just before he died. He was a prominent figure at the post World War II and international order-establishing Bretton Woods Conference held in 1944 in the United States. Though he was not the main force behind the World Bank and International Monetary Fund agencies, he definitely played a role in the financial architecture of the world this conference established. The final major public role he carried out lay in his successful negotiation for Britain of a multiple billion dollar loan from its war ally the United States in 1945. Keynes died the next year.

Key Performance Indicator (KPI)

Key Performance Indicators are measurements that aid companies and other organizations in assessing the progress they are making towards their key goals. It is important for any organization to start out by deciding on its mission and determining its goals. Once they have done this effectively, they can decide on the best means of measuring their incremental progress to reaching the goals.

A characteristic of Key Performance Indicators is that they are measurements that are quantifiable. They must also be relevant to the organization's particular benchmarks of success. These will be different for various organizations. A business and a community service organization will not have the same KPIs.

Businesses could have KPIs that relate to their total profits or amount of income that they derive from repeat customers. Customer service departments could use KPIs that measure the number of calls they answer in under a minute. Schools' Key Performance Indicators could center on the percentages of students who graduate. Community service organizations might look at a KPI that revolves around the number of individuals they are able to assist in a given year.

There is no one right or wrong Key Performance Indicator. KPIs only need to be measurable, relevant to the goals of the organization, and a core part of the group's success. As an outfit's goals evolve or are met, the KPI goals may shift as well.

Key Performance Indicators have to be definable and measurable to be useful. It is no good setting a KPI that is subjective or a matter of opinion. Their definitions also should be consistent year in and year out. This is the only way that the targets set for each KPI will be meaningful.

If a company sets a goal to be the best employer, then they might use their company Turnover Rate each year as a Key Performance Indicator. This will work so long as they are using the same turnover rate definition and measurement each year. Reducing turnover by a certain percent annually is an understandable goal that different departments can act on and address.

Another important attribute of these Key Performance Indicators is that they have to be relevant to the organization and its goals. A business whose goal is to become the most profitable company in the sector will need to use KPIs that address profits and relevant finances. They might choose profits before taxes. Schools that are not interested in turning profits would not utilize such KPIs.

For Key Performance Indicators to be helpful they also need to be a core part of an organization's success. KPIs are only practical so long as they relate to the elements that the organization needs to work on so that they can attain the goals. Another important facet of these KPIs is that there should not be too many of them.

The idea is for the members of the organization to be able to focus on the identical Key Performance Indicators. It is possible for the organization as a whole to have three to five KPIs while departments have several others that help to support the overall goals. So long as these goals can be neatly categorized under the company's larger ones, this is acceptable.

Key Performance Indicators make a good tool for performance management. When everyone in the organization is aware of the goals, then they can take appropriate steps to help reach them. KPIs can be posted on company websites, in employee break rooms, and in company conference rooms. All of the activities of the members of the organization should be focused towards meeting or even surpassing those KPI goals.

Keynesian Economics

Keynesian economics represents a system of economic ideas that the British economist John Maynard Keynes developed in the first half of the twentieth century. Keynes became best known for his easy to understand and straight forward arguments for the underlying causes of the Great Depression.

His theories of economics found their basis in the concept of the circular flows of money. As his ideas became more and more widely accepted, they led to a range of intervening economic policies towards the end of the Great Depression, particularly in the United States.

Keynes explained all flows of money in terms of their impact on other people and entities. He said that a single person's spending contributes to the next individual's paycheck. That person spending their pay would then supply the earnings of another. This virtuous circle goes on and on and assists in maintaining a healthy economy that is working properly.

As the Great Depression settled in, the natural inclination of people to save and hold their money increased. Keynes proposed that this cessation in the normally occurring circular money flow is what caused the economies of the world to grind to a screeching halt.

More than only explaining economic problems, Keynes offered solutions as well. He claimed that the best cure for this disease lay in priming the pump. With this expression, he intended for governments to intervene in order to boost their spending. They might do this by purchasing things on the open market or by growing the money supply itself.

At the time of the Great Depression, such an answer did not turn out to be well received at first. Even so, the actions of American President Franklin D. Roosevelt in spending enormously on defense for the Second World War are generally credited for beginning the United States' economic revival.

Because Keynesian economics strongly makes the case for the government to jump in and help out the economy, it represented a serious break from the prior system of laissez-fair capitalism economics that predated it. This laissez-fair, or hands off, approach had endeavored to keep government out of the markets. The system argued that markets left undisturbed would find their own balance in time.

Keynes' ideas represented a direct challenge to the many supporters of free market capitalism, such as the Austrian School of economics. Frederick von Hayek proved to be among its earliest founders who lived in England and represented a bitter public rival to Keynes. Their ideas on government influence in private citizen's lives battled back and forth for years in public policy debate.

Keynesian economics discourages an excessive amount of savings, which it calls an insufficient amount of consumption and spending for the economy. The theory furthermore argues in favor of a great amount of redistributing wealth as necessary. Keynes thought that giving the poorest members of society money would lead to them probably spending it, which would support economic growth.

Keynesian economics has been a major force in international economic policy since World War II. Though its influence is less in the past three decades, it has not died out. Its tenets are again gaining ground in the light of the failures that led to the financial collapse and the Great Recession.

Local Money

Local Money is money that is created, printed, issued, and traded by an individual community. Communities that are struggling to keep their economies going are in need of a way of boosting the local economic picture. In creating money that can only be utilized by individuals and businesses in their own local area, they attempt to address this problem.

In the United States, local money's history originated in the difficult era of the Great Depression. During this decade of the 1930's, banks were failing in numbers not seen before. This created a real shortage of currency and loans in local communities and towns. Individuals and businesses worked together to find a solution to the problem. They teamed up and created their own currencies that became known as Scrip. Utilizing this newly created local Scrip, trade and exchange continued to go on even with a shortage of banks and hard currency in the smaller towns throughout America.

Today's local money concept has made a comeback in the wake of the financial crisis and the Great Recession. Businesses began working with area banks to come up with their own local currency that could be purchased and issued to consumers in the area. In communities where local money has arisen again, a great number of businesses have signed on to the idea and consented to taking payment in the bills of this localized currency money. This is necessary in order for area consumers to feel compelled to obtain the local money in the first place.

The way that local money works in practice today is interesting. The currency is printed up and then offered by area banks in a participating community. The currency is then sold at a significant discount to its actual value. For example, $100 local money could be sold by area banks for only $95 United States dollars. The $100 local money can then by spent by the consumer at its full value in any business that takes the local money as a method of payment.

Already, over a dozen area communities throughout the U.S. have created their own local money currencies that are being honored on a fairly large scale. Not only is this helping out area businesses by keeping the locally earned paychecks in the communities, but since the currencies are sold at a five to ten percent discount to dollars, it allows struggling workers and families to stretch their incomes by using them. In communities that honor local money, they can be utilized to pay for groceries, gasoline, and even Yoga classes, as examples. Among the more successful and widely accepted local monies these days are the Ithaca Hours of Ithaca, New York; the BerkShares in Western Massachusetts; and the Detroit Cheers in Detroit, Illinois.

The BerkShares for Western Massachusetts are a model case study of successful local money. They can be purchased from twelve banks throughout the area. BerkShares are accepted at in excess of three hundred seventy different businesses in the region. As the largest local money network in the U.S, the BerkShares have so far circulated almost two and a half million dollars. Successes like these have encouraged other communities like South Bend, Indiana to begin creating their own local currency.

Ludwig von Mises

Ludwig von Mises turned out to be among the very last thinkers of the original epoch of the Austrian School of Economics. He obtained his law and economics doctorate late in the period of the Austrian School in 1906 at the University of Vienna. His writings and teaching had a tremendous impact on the young people of his day and age, especially Americans of that and future generations.

The Theory of Money and Credit proved to be among the best and most influential of Ludwig von Mises' works. This ground breaking work became published in 1912. It served as a principal banking and monetary textbook for fully the following two decades. In this influential work, von Mises took off on the Austrian marginal utility theory to expand the idea to money. He observed that no one demands money simply to possess money for its intrinsic nature. Instead, individuals are attracted to its utility in buying goods with it. This was revolutionary thought at the time.

In the book, Ludwig von Mises also postulated that the business cycles of economies occur because governments allow limitless expansion of credit by the banks. Mises then went on to put his ideas into place by founding his Austrian Institute for Business Cycle Research in 1926.

The students of Ludwig von Mises were many and some of them were important to later generations. Friedrich Hayek became the most influential of them. He eventually expanded and extrapolated further on Mises' ideas on business cycles.

Besides these important ideas, Ludwig von Mises made other important contributions to the fields of political and economic thought. He argued that socialism would fall because its economy collapsed first. He penned a 1920 article which postulated social governments would be unable to engage in the necessary economic calculations which were needful in order to establish complicated and efficient economies. Social economists of the time Abba Lerner and Oskar Lange vehemently disagreed with his arguments. Today the majority of economists side with von Mises and his arguments which were further expounded on by his star pupil Hayek.

Ludwig von Mises felt certain that self-evident axioms made economic truths in practice. These economic principals were not able to be tested empirically he believed. Finally he reached the point of writing his magnum opus great work entitled *Human Action*. In this and other publications, he spelled out his full world view of economics and human interaction. Unfortunately at the time, von Mises was unable to persuade the majority of economists living in his age who were outside of the Austrian School of Economics. He strongly championed laissez-faire economics, arguing that the government had no place to be involved in any portion of a national economy. There were points where he violated his own rules with some important exceptions. He believed that war justified forced military conscription, a sharply anti-free market idea.

Ludwig von Mises served as a professor without pay for the University of Vienna during the years 1913 through 1934. He worked officially for the Vienna Chamber of Commerce as economist at the same time. While in this role, he labored on behalf of the Austrian national government as their main economic advisor. When Nazism took root in his native Austria, von Mises immigrated to Geneva, Switzerland in 1934. There he became professor in the Graduate Institute of International Studies. He served in this capacity until he eventually immigrated on to New York City in the U.S. in 1940. He worked as a visiting profess there in New York University from 1945 through his eventual retirement in 1969.

Sadly for Ludwig von Mises, his economic policy ideas were out of political favor policy wise in the years of the Keynesian revolution which swept across the American elite and political landscape between the 1930s and the 1960s. He became increasingly bitter after Hitler wrecked the land of his birth and as the Keynesian ideas became a full blown revolution in Washington D.C., London, and Paris. He went full circle from believing himself to be a mainstream member of economics to a final dismal view of himself as an economic outcast. This is evident in his book *The Theory of Money and Credit*. In the early sections he wrote in 1912, he argues calmly and rationally, while in the final section penned in the 1940s, he is vehement and argumentative.

Despite this pitiful end to his great life and work, Von Mises had a profound legacy, especially in the United States. His powerful impact on the young people of his generation and that of his successor Hayek caused the Austrian School of Economics to enjoy a powerful resurgence in the U.S.

after his death.

Maastricht Treaty

The Maastricht Treaty is the main treaty of the European Union. It was originally known as the TEU Treaty on European Union. This agreement was signed in Maastricht, the Netherlands on February 7, 1992. Members of the European Community debated it in their individual countries and then signed it. The treaty came about as an effort to fully integrate Europe into a closer political and economic union.

The treaty established the European Union. It also set the groundwork for creating the euro, the single currency of the EU. The Maastricht Treaty was subsequently amended by several other agreements. These included the Amsterdam, Nice, and Lisbon treaties.

This treaty represented a significant milestone in the process of integrating Europe. It modified other previously signed agreements like the treaties of Paris and Rome, as well as the Single European Act. These earlier arrangements had economic goals for the community. The original stated objective had been to create a common market for trading and investment.

With the Maastricht Treaty, the Europeans signed on to a spelled out vision of political union for the first time. After the treaty came into effect, the European project no longer went under the name of European Economic Community or EEC. Instead, it became known as the EU or European Union. Article 2 in this treaty called for "the process of creating an ever closer union among the peoples of Europe."

This Maastricht Treaty had a structural base of three pillars. The central pillar referred to the community dimension. It set out arrangements that pertained to common community policies, citizenship in the EU, and economic and monetary union. These were laid out in the Euratom, the ECSC, and the EC treaties. This pillar led to the eventual creation of the European Central Bank and the euro.

The second pillar concerned the CFSP Common foreign and security policy. Under this idea, the countries of the European Union would create a foreign minister for the EU to represent their single voice and policy objectives overseas. They also began working to come up with a common defensive policy with the intention of eventually creating an EU military force. This pillar also pertains to immigration and border control issues. It has suffered a serious challenge since the European refugee crisis has brought more than a million mostly Syrian and Iraqi refugees across the external borders of the E.U.

The third pillar of the Maastricht Treaty is the idea that there would be police and judicial cooperation. This pertained to criminal issues and concerns. It established a European Court of Justice whose decisions supersede those of the national country high courts.

The Maastricht Treaty also laid the grounds for the creation of the European Commission and the European Parliament. These bodies govern many budgetary and even political affairs within the block.

The Maastricht Treaty set in motion the discontent that led to the Brexit vote and the United Kingdom's decision to leave the EU. The pillars on common security and judicial cooperation turned out to major sore points with the British people. On the one hand, they despised the loss of control over their immigration policy and borders.

On the other they did not like the fact that they had also lost judicial control. A number of high profile court cases decided in the highest British court were subsequently overturned by the European Court of Justice. This all helped to explain why the majority of the British voted against the ever further political union which article two of the treaty established.

Macroeconomics

Macroeconomics refers to the division within economics that concentrates its study on the workings of large national economies, or even regional economies, in their entirety. This field proves to be extremely general as a result.

It is mostly concerned with big picture measurements like the rates of unemployment, as well as with the developing of models whose purpose is to detail the various indicators' correlations. An opposite to macroeconomics might be said to be microeconomics that focuses on the activities of individuals and businesses instead of bigger pictures and scales. Macroeconomics and microeconomics are considered to be complimentary studies.

Because of the Great Depression that occurred in the 1930's, the study of macroeconomics evolved into a practical area of economics on which economists might concentrate their efforts. Up to that point, economists did not distinguish between the activities of individuals and businesses and an entire national economy. The most influential developers of macroeconomics proved to be those economists who made it their business to relate what had caused the Great Depression. The British economist John Maynard Keynes is among the chief of these economists who developed the study.

Until just a few decades ago, Keynes' ideas on macroeconomics overshadowed the entire field. Followers of Keynesian thought depended on the concept of aggregate demand, or total demand, to grapple with hard questions in macroeconomics, like the way to explain what stood behind particular unemployment levels. Today, Keynesian models are not the underlying philosophy of macroeconomics any longer, as neoclassical economics has successfully challenged it. Still, the presently used models bear great influence of the Keynesian precursors.

To date, no one economic philosophy has come up with a single model that is able to correctly and totally reproduce the ways that economies literally work. This causes different economists to have varying understandings of economics. Because of this, gaining an understanding of macroeconomics involves studying the ideas of each major economic school of thought.

As a result of the field of macroeconomics, governments have taken proactive approaches to managing economic cycles and changes. They do this through governmental policies that are utilized to create changes with the goals of either avoiding or lessening the impacts of economic shocks, such as depressions. This management of large national economies is affected in practical terms through two types of government policies. These are monetary and fiscal policies. Monetary policies involve the governmental control of the nation's money supply and the national interest rate levels. Their goals are both stable prices with low inflation and low unemployment levels.

Fiscal policies are amounts of spending that a government engages in, as well as taxes that they collect, to influence the economy. For example, the government can expand the economy by spending a good deal more money than it collects in tax revenues. It might similarly contract economic activity by spending less money than it actually brings in from taxes. Besides this, a government can stimulate the economy by cutting tax rates, or shrink the economic activity levels by raising tax rates.

Market Failure

Market failure refers to a scenario where rational behavior does not prevail and lead to optimal economic outcomes for the group involved. This break down occurs because the individual incentives are insufficient to lead the participants to do what is best for the greater common good.

When such failure happens, every person will still make the ideal choices for himself or herself, but these will turn out to be the incorrect choices for the group as a whole. This is a function of microeconomics. It is depicted as a steady state disequilibrium where the amount supplied is not sufficient to match the amount demanded.

Such market failure transpires as individuals representing a group end up with a worse outcome than if they had not engaged in decisions that resulted in their own best interests. These groups end up with fewer benefits or pay costs which are too high. This sounds like an easy to understand idea, yet it is often deceptive and thus can be misidentified.

The name is a misnomer itself. It has nothing to do with any intrinsic problems within the market economy construct. Market failures could occur within government sponsored activities just as easily. A classic example surrounds those groups with special interests that are looking for affordable rents. These groups are able to obtain an outsized influence by lobbying government for costs on everyone outside of their own group, such as with tariffs. As other small groups are able to impose their own higher costs, the entire population proves to be in a poorer state than if no one had lobbied the government in the first place.

Another difference has to do with results. Not every negative outcome that results from market activity is classified properly as a market failure. These failures also do not mean that actors in the private marketplace are not able to address and resolve the problem themselves either. At the same time, all market failures do not have a possible solution. This is the case even when the public has been made aware of the problem or a sensible law is in effect.

A number of typical types of market failures exist. Among the most frequently mentioned are monopoly privileges, externalities, factor immobility, and information asymmetries. The so called "public good problem" represents a simple to grasp example. These public goods refer to services or goods where the maker is not able to limit the amount of consumption to those customers who pay.

Market failures can occur with public goods when there are consumers in the market place who choose to utilize the goods but refuse to pay. National Defense is a classic example of this as a service that benefits all citizens whether they pay or not. No one could practically produce the best quality and quantity of national defense on a private basis. Governments similarly are not able to employ a competitive pricing system to ascertain the right amount of national defense. This represents a classic market failure for which there is no definitive solution.

Solutions to a number of potential market failures exist. Information which is asymmetrical can be addressed using ratings agencies like Standard & Poor's or Moody's to detail risks of securities. In the world of electronics, this service is provided by Underwriter's Laboratories LLC. Negative externalities like pollution can be handled by lawsuits that make it more expensive for the polluter to operate this way.

Microeconomics

Microeconomics is an economic social science that examines the results of individual human behavior. Unlike the big picture macroeconomics, it is most concerned with how peoples' choices impact distribution and utility of scarce economic resources. The science demonstrates and explains the ways that various goods possess different values from each other. It also considers how people engage in more productive and efficient decisions and how they can work together most effectively. This science has long been regarded as a better settled and more advanced one than macroeconomics.

Microeconomics studies economic tendencies. This means it considers what will occur when people pursue particular choices or as production factors change in some way. It categorizes the actors according to microeconomic divisions such as sellers, buyers, and owners of businesses. Such participants engage with supply and demand in order to obtain resources. They employ both interest rates and money as means for coordinating pricing.

Microeconomics does not attempt to reveal the way a market should work. Rather it is interested in describing what will occur if specific conditions alter. As an example, a car maker might increase the cost of its vehicles. This science states that buyers will purchase a smaller number of them after the price increase. Similarly, if silver mines in Peru are shut down, supply will be constrained and the global silver prices will likely rise. The study is able to explain why slower sales of smart watches will tend to make Apple's stock fall. It can also describe how an increase in the minimum wage will lead Burger King to put on fewer employees. It leaves the future levels of gross domestic product of countries in the European Union to macroeconomics.

Microeconomic study typically follows Leon Walras' general equilibrium theory as described in his 1874 "Elements of Pure Economics" and Alfred Marshall's partial equilibrium theory from his 1890 work "Principles of Economics." Their methods seek to distill the behavior of people down to a language of functional mathematics. This way economists can come up with a model for individual markets that can be tested mathematically.

Their methods fit in with the neoclassical microeconomic umbrella. Followers of the neoclassical view believe that economists can create hypotheses for economic events which are quantifiable and can apply empirical evidence to determine which function best. The efficiency of the models is decided by how effectively real world markets fall into place according to a given model's rules.

There is one substantial alternative view within the study of microeconomics. This is the Austrian school followers' ideas. They disregard the ides of static equilibrium espoused by the neoclassical view as irreparably flawed. They choose instead to use logical deduction as the basis for their analysis.

Their two principles are subjective conditions and spontaneous order. Their model explains the way that economic incentives allow people to overcome uncertainty and lack of knowledge. They would claim that markets happen because individuals possess varying interests and preferences and an imperfect knowledge. Markets allow people to overcome these handicaps, according to proponents of the Austrian school.

Middle Class

In the United States, the Middle Class is a broadly defined social group found throughout America. There are no exact definitions of what comprises the middle class. Depending on whose standard you use, the middle class in the U.S. is made up of from twenty-five to sixty-six percent of families.

The middle class in America have been responsible for many of the country's greatest accomplishments. Middle class people are known by characteristics of creativity, coming up with concepts, and consultative abilities. Most middle class people have either obtained a college degree or at least been through some years of college education.

Middle class values are central to the recognized American way of life. These values center around sticking to intrinsically held ethics and beliefs, independence, and innovation. Middle class people prove to be more politically motivated and active than do the other demographics throughout American society.

The income of the middle class ranges widely. It can be from around the national median income to over $100,000 per year. This means that the standard of living for middle class people can similarly vary greatly, dependent on the size of the household in question. This means that families with two incomes that have many members can earn more than a smaller family in the upper middle class that only has one income, even though the latter's standard of living would be considerably higher.

The middle class in the United States remains the most influential group in American society. They are responsible for the vast majority of teachers, writers, voters, editors, and journalists. The majority of trends within the United States begin with the middle class.

The middle class also pay the majority of the taxes within the U.S., making them an extremely critical group economically. The top twenty-five percent of earners, the overwhelming majority of whom are considered to be middle class, pay eighty-five percent of all taxes in the United States. Meanwhile, the bottom fifty percent pay only three percent, while the wealthiest one percent pay up to thirty-seven percent of the total share of taxes.

Even though the Middle Class are considered to be indispensable to American society and the economy, their ranks are dwindling with time. Data on income demonstrates that the American Middle Class have benefited from much slower growth in income than the top one percent of wealthy wage earners, according to data going back to 1980. This stands in contrast to the rise in income seen in the years after World War II, when the income of the middle class grew at the same pace as did the income of the rich. In the years since then, the rich have out gained the middle class considerably.

As an example, from 1979 to 2005, the after tax earnings of the top one percent grew inflation adjusted by 176% as opposed to only sixty-nine percent for the top twenty percent of wage earners as a whole and only twenty-nine percent for the top forty percent of workers. As a percentage of total gross yearly household income, the top one percent currently make over nineteen percent of all earnings, representing their greatest share of the wealth since the late 1920's.

Further proof that the critical middle class is shrinking is revealed by the June 2006 Brookings Institution survey. It demonstrated that the neighborhoods of middle income Americans as a percent of all metropolitan neighborhoods have decline dramatically over a thirty year period. From 1970 to 2000, this percentage decreased from fifty-eight percent to forty-one percent. According to this data, the middle class have already fallen well below the significant half of the country's population that it always represented in the past.

Monetary Policy

This is one of the two tools the government has to influence the overall economy. With monetary policy, a nation's central bank takes action to influence the economy. In the United States, the Federal Reserve Board is the central bank. They regulate the interest rates and money supply available in the country to stabilize the national currency and to control inflation. Monetary policy is the sister policy to fiscal policy.

Monetary policy is effective because the Federal Reserve or other central bank is able to change the real cost of money. This allows them to influence business and consumer spending behavior and the amount of money they use. With this policy, central banks are able to mange their nation's money supply. It allows them to oversee stable economic growth.

The money supply is made up of several components. These include cash, checks, credit, and money market funds. Credit is among the most important and biggest categories of money supply. It covers mortgages, loans, bonds, and other promises to repay.

There are two goals in which central banks utilize monetary policy. They are attempting to manage inflation levels and to lower unemployment rates. The United States Federal Reserve maintains particular target ranges in these two goals.

The Fed desires its core inflation rates to be around 2% and no higher than 2.5%. They are seeking to keep unemployment rates under 6.5%. The U.S. believes a healthy unemployment rate ranges from 4.7% to 5.8%. On top of this, the Federal Reserve is looking for steady rates of economic growth. By this they mean a yearly increase of from 2% to 3% in the Gross Domestic Product.

There are two types of monetary policies from which central banks can choose. They use expansionary monetary policy to increase economic growth. Central banks decrease interest rates, increase liquidity to the markets, and purchase securities from their member banks to affect this.

Central banks employ contractionary monetary policy to slow down economic growth. They may sell securities in open market operations, increase interest rates, and increase liquidity to banks and markets in order to create this impact. Central banks have several different tools they can utilize to pursue their monetary policy. They perform open market operations by purchasing short term government bonds or selling these. Buying bonds increases the money supply while selling them decreases it.

They can also raise or lower their main interest rates like Fed Funds rate in the U.S. or LIBOR in the U.K. This changes the price at which consumers and businesses can borrow money. Cheaper money means consumers purchase bigger, longer term goods using cheap credit. Businesses pursue expansion and hire more people with cheaper priced debt. Savers are encouraged to put their money into stocks and securities to earn higher returns than savings accounts pay when interest rate are low.

Central banks can also change the reserve requirements that banks must keep. Higher reserves reduce their ability to make loans and help to decrease inflation. Lower reserves allow them to make more loans but drive inflation higher.

Since the Great Recession in 2008, different central banks have engaged in more unconventional monetary policy in an effort to kick start declining economies. Quantitative Easing has been among these policies. It involves buying financial assets from banks with money the central banks print.

From 2008 to 2013 the U.S. Federal Reserve massively expanded its balance sheet by trillions of dollars by purchasing mortgage backed securities and Treasury notes. Encouraged by the relative success and so far limited consequences of these actions, the Bank of England, the Bank of Japan, and European Central Bank have also engaged in their own quantitative easing policies. Critics have warned that such quantitative easing will massively increase inflation at some point in the future.

Money of Zero Maturity (MZM)

Money of zero maturity represents a way of measuring the money supply. This measurement for money which is circulating in an economy only covers money that is available to be spent and utilized. As such, this MZM is really a counting of all of the money supply that is liquid in a given economy.

Individuals can figure up the money of zero maturity with some basic math. This starts with obtaining the M2 measure of the money supply. From this M2 figure, all time deposits must be subtracted, such as with certificates of deposit. Next this result must be taken and added to the amount of money market funds which are available. This sum finally provides the MZM.

In practical terms, this measure of money includes several different components. All physical currency, including bank notes and coins, are a part of it. Checking account balances are also included. Savings account totals similarly comprise the MZM. Finally, money market accounts round out the figure. These are all configurations of money which are immediately available for par value to both companies and individuals.

Other forms of money are not included in the measure. Money of zero maturity never considers money held in accounts such as certificates of deposit or any other types of time deposits. This is because these funds contained in such financial instruments can not be instantly accessed for full par value. Similarly investments held in stocks and bonds must be first sold and settled before they can be obtained.

A number of analysts like to utilize the money of zero maturity because it proves to be an extremely liquid measurement. In fact this has grown to become among the most preferred means of measuring the country's money supply exactly because it does more completely depict the readily available money in the economy that can be employed for consumption and other spending. The name for this money measure comes from its combination of all available liquid and money with zero maturity that the three M's contain in M1, M2, and M3.

There are practical applications for the money of zero maturity measurement. The figure presents a reliable indicator of a nation's actual money base for the entire economy. As such it depicts the quantity of money which is literally moving throughout the economy as a whole. Since the Federal Reserve quit tracking and following the M3 number for money supply back in 2006 on March 23rd, this has become a preferred measurement of money supply, if not the most popular one.

When economists and analysts are aware of the amount of money which is moving throughout the economy, they can develop a feeling for two important trends. They are able to learn at a fairly quick glance whether or not the economy is growing or is instead contracting. By studying this figure, they can also determine how high the danger for inflation is over the near term.

When economists look at a chart of the MZM, they are interested in the rate of growth on a year to year, quarter to quarter, or month to month basis. As this growth rate improves, the economy is likely to expand along with it, and the threat of inflation increases apace. If instead the growth rate in the MZM decreases, the economy stands a solid chance of shrinking. This would mean inflationary threats are lower.

MoneyGram

Money Gram is the name of the money transfer firm headquartered within the U.S. in Dallas, Texas. Its full name is MoneyGram International. The company's operations center is located in St. Louis Park, Minnesota. The corporation maintains both regional and locally based offices throughout the globe.

The company divides its various businesses along the lines of two different groups. These are Global Funds Transfers and Financial Paper Products. Using its proprietary network of financial institution clients and agents found around the world, the firm assists both businesses and individuals in transferring money and with various financial paper instruments.

As the number two biggest money transfer service in the world, Money Gram is second only to Western Union. The firm does business in over 200 nations and possesses a worldwide network equating to approximately 347,000 agent offices.

The creation of Money Gram International occurred because two independent businesses merged. This was the Travelers Express of Minneapolis, Minnesota and Integrated Payment Systems of Denver, Colorado. Integrated Payment Systems first set up Money Gram as a subsidiary unit. They spun it off into an independent firm which Travelers then acquired in 1998. By 2004, Travelers Express had opted to change its name to today's MoneyGram International.

The Global Funds Transfers division covers two services. These are the MoneyGram Money Transfer service and the MoneyGram Bill Payments Services. The bill payment group helps individuals to effect rapid payments as well as to pay normally occurring bills to various creditors.

The Financial Paper Products division vends several financial payment instruments. These include Money Orders and Official Checks. The Money Orders group represents the second biggest supplier of such money orders in the world. As an official check provider, Money Gram provides outsourcing services for bank checks to financial institutions, such as banks located within the United States. Such official checks are required by individual consumers if their payee needs a bank check or cashiers check that is actually drawn on the bank. Financial institutions also utilize them to pay their own bills.

In 1996, Integrated Payment Systems evolved into its own publically traded corporation. As such it was already the second biggest non banking consumer money transfer operation in the U.S. The company renamed itself MoneyGram Payment Systems Inc. as part of the spin off into independence. Rapid growth of the new corporation occurred under the leadership of James Calvano who came to the new company in 1997. He had formerly been the Western Union President before moving to the Chief Executive Officer role at MoneyGram Payment Systems.

It was in 1997 that MoneyGram Payment Systems Inc opted to change its name yet again to MoneyGram International Limited. When MoneyGram International arose, the company had two owners. MoneyGram Payment systems controlled the group with 51 percent stake in the renamed firm. Largest British travel agent firm in the world the Thomas Cook Group owned the remaining 49 percent.

In the year 2003, Travelers Express entered the picture by obtaining 100 percent ownership of the MoneyGram International and MoneyGram network. Travelers Express recognized the power of the MoneyGram brand name and changed its own name to MoneyGram International Inc in January of 2004. By the year 2006, this firm had grown overseas to comprise more than 96,000 individual agents. Their network now covered such high growth regions as Eastern Europe, Asia-Pacific, and Central America.

MoneyGram was nearly destroyed during the Global Financial Crisis of 2007-2009. The company suffered losses of $1.6 billion in 2008 because of its various investments in mortgage backed securities which turned out to be highly risky instruments. The firm had to sell a controlling interest to Goldman Sachs and Thomas H. Lee Partners then in order to receive a desperately needed cash infusion to continue ongoing operations.

As the company was in limbo, U.S. Bancorp moved their money transfer business services over to rival largest money transfer company in the world (and financially far more stable) Western Union. By 2009, MoneyGram had stabilized and returned to profitability. The company agreed to be acquired by Ant Financial Services Group on January 26th of 2017, pending regulatory approval.

National Bureau of Economic Research (NBER)

The NBER National Bureau of Economic Research is an organization whose purpose centers on creating and disbursing economic research. They are committed to encouraging better understanding of the way the economy functions for individuals, businesses, and policymakers. As part of this they write and distribute unbiased economic reports.

The NBER got its start in 1920 as a not for profit, private, non-political group. Their objectives from the start were undertaking research on economics and sharing it with business people, politicians, and academics. The researchers who are connected with NBER study a great range of different economic and business subjects.

Along with this they utilize numerous research methods in their studies. The group focuses on numerous different topics. Chief among them are creating quantitative economic behavior models, coming up with new ways to measure statistics, and studying the impacts that public policies cause.

The history of the NBER shows they covered many important ground breaking economic issues within American society. Their early efforts centered on longer term growth for the economy, the full business cycle, and the aggregate economy. In the formative years Wesley Mitchell wrote an important paper about the business cycle. Simon Kuznets pioneered the topic of national income accounting.

Milton Friedman researched and argued for money demand and what determined consumer spending. All of these proved to be in the earlier studies performed by the National Bureau of Economic Research. In 1984, Solomon Fabricant wrote a summary of their initial work and development entitled Toward a Firmer Basis of Economic Policy: The Founding of the National Bureau of Economic Research.

The NBER has greatly expanded and grown in influence over the years. Today it is considered to be the foremost group for not for profit research on economics in the United States. Among the economists who were affiliated with NBER are 25 Nobel Prize winners. There have also been 13 heads of the Presidential Council of Economic Advisers among their affiliated members.

NBER researchers today include over 1,400 business and economics professors who teach throughout universities and colleges around the U.S. and Canada. These researching scholars are considered to be the leaders within their own fields. The vast majority of those researchers who hold NBER affiliation have a title of RA Research Associates or FRF Faculty Research Fellows. These Research Associates are tenured by their home university or college. Their appointments to this senior status must be NBER Board of Directors approved. Faculty Research Fellows usually prove to be junior scholars in their fields.

The NBER does not receive direct tax dollar support. It operates based on a variety of research grants. These supporting grants come from private foundations, government agencies, corporate and individual contributions, and investment income.

The NBER is well organized and run by a board of directors that governs it. Its headquarters are based in Cambridge, Massachusetts. The group also maintains a branch office in New York City. The members of this board come from and represent both important national economics entities and foremost American researching universities. The board also hosts members who are important economists at academia, trade unions, and corporations. Being a board member of this national economics group is a prestigious honor.

In 2016 the Chief Executive Officer and President of the NBER is James Poterba. He is served by 45 personnel who staff the organization. These employees are besides the Faculty Research Fellows and Research Associates located around North America. The research group is governed by various important documents. These include their NBER by-laws, incorporation certificate, and the conflict of interest policy for directors and officers.

Negative Income Tax

A negative income tax is a tax regime that is considered to be extremely progressive. In this system, those individuals who earn less than a minimum specified amount obtain additional income from their government rather than have to pay the government taxes into the system at all.

This type of forward thinking system has been bandied about by various economists over the years and yet never fully realized in a developed economy. In the 1940's, British politician Juliet Rhys-Williams became among the first to make the political discussion serious. In the 1960's in the United States, American legendary free market economist Milton Friedman became a major proponent of the idea.

The function of a negative income tax can be two fold. It can institute a minimum income level. It might also be utilized to provide supplemental income to families earning too little to survive. In this capacity, it would serve the function of providing a system with a guaranteed income minimum.

In such a negative income tax regime, those individuals who bring home a particular income amount would not pay any taxes. Others who earn over this threshold would then pay a percentage of the income they earned over that pre-determined level. Those individuals on the margins of society who realized incomes lower than this amount would receive payments to supplement at least a part of their income shortfall. The amount of money by which their income was below that pre-set level would equal in theory the amount of payments they received from the government and its taxing authority.

In 1962, renowned American economist Milton Friedman first seriously put forward the plan for a guaranteed minimum income in the United States. He envisioned a nation where subsidies provided in the form of federal income would be dealt out to families or individuals whose income was lower than a minimum level.

This negative income tax would ensure that potential claimants could simply and easily obtain the money by filling out their annual tax returns instead of having to apply for and receive welfare benefits. The advantage to such a system would be that it eliminated more or less the requirements of having a complicated welfare system bureaucracy.

Despite the income distribution benefits for the poor that a negative income tax system offers, it is not without its substantial share of vocal critics. This main critique stems from the fact that some low income workers would be discouraged from working at all when on this system. The reason is because if the government will provide one with $2,500 per year without working at all when the individual might only earn $5,000 annually in working dozens of hours per week, many consumers would opt instead to not work at all. They would prefer to enjoy the leisure time which they could spend working, even if this means that they ultimately might have a smaller amount of money which was insufficient to cover their essential costs of living.

Another criticism centers on accountability and potential abuse of such a negative income tax system. These critics argue that it is impossible to completely eliminate a large and costly welfare system infrastructure by doling out negative income tax payments. The other taxpayers who are in effect paying for the subsidies will insist on accountability being instituted for those citizens who are receiving what are ultimately subsidies from their income. Such a demand would necessitate a complicated combination of oversight and rules that were necessary to stop possible abuses of the negative income-welfare system.

Negative Interest Rates

Negative interest rates are those that fall below 0%. In the past, negative interest proved to be only a theoretical discussion that economists played around with for the sake of argument. In 2010 Sweden's central bank put these rates into practice as a means of stemming the flow of outside money into the country. Denmark followed suite in 2012. Since then, minor to major central banks have moved into the mostly uncharted waters of these negative rates.

The reason that central banks would be interested in such negative interest rates is that they help the economy. Central banks cutting the rates into negative territory creates a similar effect as simply lowering interest rates. Lower rates help consumers to spend and businesses to invest more.

They also boost prices in the stock markets and other risk assets. They reduce the level of the nation's currency. This helps exports to be more competitive against other country's goods. Finally lower rates cause people to expect higher inflation rates in the future. This encourages consumers to spend their money now as opposed to later when it will be worth less.

The world has many decades of knowledge of what happens when central banks influence economies by reducing rates from 3% to 2% because of downturns in the economy. In theory this shifting to negative interest rates is similar with the difference of a starting point at or below zero.

Such NIRP negative interest rate policies are called unconventional monetary tools. The idea is to move benchmark interest rates into negative territory. Doing so means breaking the centuries' long barrier of 0%.

Deflation is what caused desperate central banks to pursue these negative interest rates and policies. In times where deflation pervades an economy, the businesses and consumers tend to hold their money rather than invest and spend it. Eventually this creates a reduction in total demand that in turn causes prices to fall even more. Output and production slow down and unemployment increases as a result.

Stagnation like this is typically avoided when central banks pursue a loose monetary policy. The problem arises when the deflation becomes so powerful that dropping interest rates to zero is no longer enough to encourage lending and borrowing.

The result of negative interest rates is profound. Central banks charge their commercial banks money (negative interest) in order to keep their deposits at the bank. Commercial banks then pass along these costs to their larger account holders as they are able. The financial institutions have not much stooped to official negative rates on their depositors. Instead they charge fees for keeping money in these current accounts. This amounts to negative rates under the guise of a different name.

Central banks hope that the commercial banks will loan out money instead of paying to hold it. Instead many banks have been paying the fees themselves, and this has impacted bank profits. Banks fear passing along fees to small deposit account holders who may withdraw their money instead.

As of 2016, the negative interest rate policy has been adopted by the European Central Bank, the Swiss National Bank, and the Bank of Japan besides the Scandinavian Central Banks. Early evidence suggests that the Euro zone did manage to reduce interbank loans with the negative interest rates. Companies have not so far much benefited from the negative interest rates. This is because the risk is perceived to be higher with corporations who borrow than with governments. One notable exception is with Nestle the Swiss food conglomerate that has issued negative interest rate corporate bonds.

Nielson

Nielson Holdings PLC represents the British-based, truly global data, information, and measurement firm which was originally started in the United States. Today it operates in more than 100 countries around the world and counts 44,000 staff among its worldwide employees. In 2015, they announced aggregate revenues of $6.2 billion. As a company with enormous operations in the U.S., it is listed on the NYSE New York Stock Exchange and the London Stock Exchange. The company is presently an S&P 500 component.

For 2016, the American Marketing Association named Nielson as its top firm out of the top 50 Market Research Firms active in the United States. Arthur C. Nielson, Sr. originally founded Nielson back in 1923. He remains famous for his invention of the idea to measure competitive sales which led to the concept of “market share.” He receives credit for coining and making famous this phrase that is ubiquitous within the United States and developed world today.

Though the company existed separately in the United States and Europe (where it traded and was headquartered initially in the Netherlands), a merger of the two sister companies in August of 2015 led to the creation of the present day (sole surviving) version of the unified company Nielson Holdings PLC based in London. The cross border merger allowed by the European Cross-Border Merger Directive allowed for this combination to occur.

Today’s Nielson Holdings remains headquartered in the United Kingdom in both England and Wales. Nielson has become the leading, multinational, independent data and measurement firm of consumer behavior, quick-selling consumer goods, and media. Its presence in over 100 countries means that its reach extends to over 90 percent of the world’s population and total GDP. Nielson delivers an exhaustive understanding of what consumers are looking at in advertising and programming to its customers. It also reveals what they purchase in products, brand names, and categories on a local, domestic, regional, and global scale and how these choices meet and intersect. As such, the firm is active in both developed and emerging markets throughout the world.

It is interesting that the Nielson brand is usually thought of in connection with its famous Nielson TV ratings. Yet as a percentage of the company's revenues and business it only comprises about a quarter of the total. The company has labored for years to simplify the organization of its vast and far flung, diverse business enterprises. As a result of these intensive efforts, they have reorganized their business lines along two reporting divisions. These are "Buy," the consumer purchasing analytics and measurement division, and "Watch," the media audience analytics and measurement division.

The Buy division represents around 55 percent of this global behemoth's revenues. It mainly assists retailers, packaged goods makers, and Wall Street analysts with understanding the interests and purchases of consumers in broad categories and specific products and brands. The aim of this division is to gather and measure all of the purchases consumers make even while their purchasing behavior is fragmenting continuously over both market segments and channels.

This division's data actually determines the amount of Diet Pepsi vs. Diet Coke and Diet Dr. Pepper which stores sell, as well as the amount of Colgate versus Crest toothpaste retailers vend. They do this in practice by buying and analyzing enormous quantities of retail data showing what the stores are selling. They combine this with their own data from household panels of surveys which gather information on what consumers bring home. This division's most important clients include Nestle, The Coca-Cola Company, Unilever Group, Procter and Gamble Company, and Wal-Mart. The buy division extends over 106 countries now, though the U.S. remains the biggest market of this division.

The other group is the Watch division. This segment represents around 45 percent of worldwide revenues. It mostly measures what consumers listen to and watch over the majority of devices and channels. This includes television, computers, radio, cell phones, over the top, and other mobile devices. As such, they measure consumers' interest in both advertising and programming over all points of distribution. They call their proprietary data measuring machine the Nielson's Total Audience Measurement system. This division's most important clients include NBC Universal, CBS, The Walt Disney Company, and News Corporation. It measures media performances in 47 nations which collectively represent around 80 percent of worldwide advertising budgets.

Nonprofit Organizations

Nonprofit Organizations represent entities whose reason for being is to provide help or value to members or the community at large. These are also called not for profit organizations as well as non-business entities. There are many reasons why an agency would incorporate as a not for profit. They are often interested in promoting points of view or social and charitable causes. Such outfits utilize excess revenues they obtain in order to promote their mission and purpose. They do not ever distribute the so-called profits to stakeholders in the form of dividend payouts. This unique feature of nonprofits is called the non-distribution limitation.

When entities elect to become a Nonprofit Organization, there will typically be tax status ramifications involved. This is the case as not for profits generally seek out tax exemption because of their charitable or socially oriented nature. It is important to note that not all NPOs are charitable organizations, even though many individuals equate the two types of organizations. It is true that charities comprise the most visible component of the category, yet many other kinds of nonprofit organizations also exist.

Founders typically design other kinds of not for profits to serve their communities or members. Among the ones which serve their communities are organizations that concentrate on delivering services to the general community on a local, national, or global scale. These could be those that provide human development and aid, human service projects and programs, health and education services, medical research benefits, and others.

Member serving nonprofit organizations include such entities as cooperatives, mutual societies, credit and trade unions, industry associations, retired servicemen's clubs, sports clubs, and advocacy or lobby groups. All of these kinds of not for profit organizations actually benefit a certain group of individuals.

With many nonprofits, they are both member-serving and community-serving at the same time. Any grassroots-based support group for cancer victims would be such an example. It serves its members who have cancer by supporting them directly. It also benefits the community at large by providing much needed services to citizens who are also members of the general public.

Though the nonprofit organizations are allowed to create additional revenues beyond their expenses, they have to keep such profit surpluses and use them for ongoing future operations, plans, or expansion efforts. They can not distribute them to any board member or director, organization participant, or beneficiary of the group.

Not for profits have one thing in common with their for profit cousins. They both have boards of directors which exercise control over their respective organizations. Both will also typically have management and other staff which receive compensation for their efforts. Some NPOs utilize executives and volunteers who are not paid or who work for a token compensation. There are jurisdictions and nations that require a nominal fee be paid to directors and managers so that they can form a legally binding contract between organization and executive or board member.

It is interesting to remember that because an organization receives the nonprofit designation, this does not signify that it will not try to turn profits. Instead it means that the entity will not have any owners who benefit from the revenues and/or profits earned. In many cases, the amounts of surplus revenues that NPOs are able to generate, keep, and even deploy are restricted by government laws and regulations within their jurisdictions.

While many nonprofit organizations are service or charitably inclined, others organize and function like a trust or a cooperative. Supporting organizations are much like NPOs. They work as a foundation yet are more complex in their administration requirements. These supporting organizations also obtain a more advantageous tax treatment and commit to restrictions on the various public charities which they support. Such an organization’s goals are not to amass wealth, but instead are to provide help for and meaning to the peoples they support.

OPEC

OPEC is the globally famous acronym for the Organization of the Petroleum Exporting Countries. This permanently standing and frequently meeting intergovernmental entity arose over fifty years ago at the Baghdad Conference held back from September 10th through the 14th of 1960. Founding meeting nations at the time were Saudi Arabia, Iraq, Iran, Kuwait, and Venezuela. These five original Founding Members later found company as nine other states joined them. These were Qatar in 1961, Libya in 1962, United Arab Emirates in 1967, Algeria in 1969, Nigeria in 1971, Ecuador in 1973, Gabon in 1975, and Angola in 2007.

Indonesia is the ninth member. They have experienced a tumultuous history recently with OPEC. The Southeast Asian nation originally joined in 1962 but suspended its membership in January of 2009. They reactivated it once again in January of 2015 then again decided to suspend membership in November of 2016.

The original headquarters of OPEC lay in Geneva, Switzerland, but only for the first five years of the organization's history. After this, the group moved the home base of operations to Vienna, Austria as of September 1, 1965. They have remained there to this day.

The objective of OPEC lies in unifying and coordinating the diverging petroleum production and sales policies of the member nations. Their goal in doing this is to ensure that petroleum prices realized by the producers are both stable and fair. They are also interested in delivering and guaranteeing an effective, uninterrupted, and economically affordable supply of petroleum and petroleum products to the wealthy consuming nations of the world. Finally, they seek a fair return on investments for those who support the industry with capital.

Their mission is nearly the same as the above defined statute. They look to make certain oil markets remain stable so that the producers are able to receive a dependable and steady income stream and consumers are able to rely on routine, economic, and efficient supplies of the crude commodity.

The formative years of OPEC in the 1960s were interesting times for the member producing states. Many of them were only achieving their independence from protectorate overlords Great Britain or France at the time. Decolonization meant that many new fully independent nations arose throughout the developing world. At the time, the world oil markets were controlled by the so called “Seven Sisters” multinational corporations. They existed almost independent from the former communist Soviet Union (the FSU) and the other communist nations of China, Vietnam, North Korea, Eastern Europe, and Cuba.

OPEC came together and refined its group vision, established their Secretariat, and created their objectives. In 1968, it adopted its “Declaratory Statement of Petroleum Policy in Member Countries.” This laid out the irrevocable rights of all nations to permanently control their own natural resources for the best interest of their own national development. By the end of the decade, OPEC had expanded to ten member states.

It was actually in the 1970s that OPEC came into its own. In this decade, they gained international notoriety as they assumed full control over their own internal petroleum industries. This allowed them to gain a huge influence over the crude oil prices on global energy markets. Thanks to their Arab oil embargo of 1973 the were able to inflict dramatic pain for national governments as well as individual consumers and businesses throughout the United States, Great Britain, and most of the wealthy developed nations of the world. By 1975, 13 countries had become members of OPEC.

Throughout the 1990s and 2000s, OPEC’s influence and great power over world oil and energy markets gradually declined as the organization fell from prominence. This happened because of ineffective coordination of policy as the years dragged on, and as other non-OPEC nations such as Norway, Great Britain, the newly revived Russia, Canada, Mexico, and the United States became major oil producers in their own rights.

Panic of 1907

The Panic of 1907 is also referred to as the Knickerbocker Crisis and the 1907 Bankers' Panic. This represented an earlier financial crisis within the United States. It occurred during a three week long time frame that began mid October of 1907 as the NYSE New York Stock Exchange plummeted nearly 50 percent from the prior year peak.

Naturally this touched off a first regional and then nationwide panic since this happened in a period of economic recession. This led to numerous runs on both national and regional banks, as well as trust companies. In time, this Panic of 1907 spread all across the country as a number of the state-chartered and local community banks as well as businesses throughout the region went into bankruptcy.

Leading causes of the panic and bank runs were due to a pull back of the market makers in the NYSE that caused liquidity from a great number of New York City banks to dry up. This led to a rapid deterioration in confidence with bank depositors. The under regulated bucket shops and side bets on the market only made matters worse.

The event which triggered the Panic of 1907 turned out to be a botched effort from October in 1907 in which speculators failed to corner the full market on the United Copper Company stock. As the bid went awry, many of the banks that had loaned out money in the cornering the stock market scheme became victims of runs on the bank that next infected affiliated trusts and banks. A week after this seminal event, the Knickerbocker Trust Company failed because of the bank runs. This represented the third biggest trust in New York City at the time of its sudden collapse.

The fall of Knickerbocker then caused fear to spread all throughout the city's many trust companies as the regional banks immediately began to withdraw their cash reserves from the New York City based banks. Throughout the U.S., panic ensued with huge numbers of savers attempting to pull out their own bank deposits from the regional and local banks. This turned quickly into a self-fulfilling prophecy.

The Panic of 1907 actually started in the summer of 1907. The American economy had already demonstrated consistent signs of weakness as a range of Wall Street-based brokers and business had declared bankruptcy. When both the Westinghouse Electric Company and Knickerbocker Trust of New York City also failed, investors spooked and began the chain reaction of events that rocked the nation in the infamous Panic of 1907.

As these critical businesses failed completely, the levels of stock markets began to collapse all the while depositors engaged in their panicked run on the country's many banks. The American Treasury Department began pumping millions of dollars into the wounded banks in a desperate effort to save them all from collapse, yet still a string of failed institutions mounted around the United States.

It was the legendary and respected J.P. Morgan who took the effective action which ultimately restored order to the markets and the national economy. He called on all of the country's important bankers and financial experts alike. They came to his home and met in his library as if it were a war room office. For three weeks, Morgan and colleagues strove to move money from the stronger banks to the weaker ones to try to provide them with a much needed lifeline to keep them financially afloat.

In the several weeks which followed, the combined efforts of J.P. Morgan and his business leader colleagues alongside that of the Treasury Department massively improved material conditions in the U.S. The crisis passed eventually and the blame game began in earnest. Reformers in both main political parties felt that the banking system of the United States had become flawed at the core and required a sea change. Roosevelt and Congress enacted some progressive banking legislation such as the Aldrich-Vreeland Act of 1908 and the Owen-Glass Federal Reserve Act of 1913 as a result. The leaders of big business became embittered as they believed that over-regulation had overturned the economy's natural rhythm.

PCE Index

The PCE Index stands for personal consumption expenditures. This economic index is used to quantify the changes in the prices of consumer services and goods. The expenditures which are included in the index are real expenditures that the U.S. government claims actual households in the U.S. spend.

The index measures data that covers non durable goods, durable goods, and services. It does share some important characteristics with the CPI Consumer Price Index, though it filters out wildly swinging commodities' prices. The Department of Commerce's Bureau of Economic Analysis includes the PCE in the personal income report which it issues.

Many officials and economists consider the PCE Index to be very predictable. This is one of the features they like about it. Other analysts favor the CPI over the PCE because they claim that it helps to discern if there is economic stability or not. CPI utilizes a fixed, set basket of goods in its calculations. The Department of Commerce likes that PCE smoothes out the inflation numbers to eliminate speculative trading based price changes in commodities.

The Federal Reserve also prefers the PCE Index to CPI. CPI may be the better known economic indicator. The Fed still chooses the PCE as its favored index as it considers the conditions in the economy. The PCE helps the American central bank to determine its plans of action which will influence employment and inflation.

The Fed has a reasoning for choosing the PCE Index. It likes the variety of expenditures which the PCE covers. CPI is more limited in utility to them precisely because its basket components are always fixed. In contrast, the PCE manages to consider a wide range of expenses that actual homes spend money on around the United States. The PCE data comes from business surveys, which are usually more reliable than those consumer based surveys that the CPI employs.

The formula of the PCE Index is also useful. It takes into account alterations in the consumers' behavior over the short term. The competing CPI does not factor in such an adjustment. All of these characteristics when taken together lead to a better rounded and all inclusive measurement of inflation. The Fed relies on the slight nuances which the PCE divulges. To them, even tiny quantities of inflation represent an economy which is healthy and expanding.

While the PCE Index breaks down to two main categories of goods and services, it subdivides the primary category of goods into two further ones. These subdivisions within goods are called durables and non durables. Durable goods refers to those which a household will be able to utilize for over three years. They come with higher price points.

In the durable goods category are televisions, cars, furniture, and refrigerators. Non durable goods are those referred to as transitory. This means that they have a life expectancy which is shorter than three years. Such items cost less and are constantly consumed. Examples of non durables include clothes, food, gasoline, and makeup.

Philanthropy

Philanthropy refers to the action of donating something. It comes from the Greek word for the love of humanity. While many people consider the term to equate to large gifts from wealthy people, this is not necessarily the case. Any type of donation is actually an act of philanthropy. This could be giving money, services, or property. It is not the amount of the donation that makes a gesture philanthropic. Instead it is the giving itself. This is equally true for a few dollars given to a person in need or several million dollars offered to an organization that is not for profit.

Philanthropy is sometimes pursued by institutions and corporations. It is most generally correlated with families or individual persons. Philanthropists are people who engage in the act of donating. This term is usually reserved for individuals who give away huge amounts of resources, as in millions. Even though individuals who give lower amounts of resources are often sacrificing more to do so, they are not usually as obvious to other people as wealthy people making contributions. This is why smaller donators seldom receive the honorific title.

Monetary donations are the most obvious forms of philanthropy. It can be given right to people who need help. Other times it is donated to charitable organizations to disperse. This category of giving can also include other financial assets like stocks or bonds. Sometimes philanthropists give these to a beloved university or research organization. A number of these donors give away their money in their will. They can provide instructions there as to what organization or group they wish it to go. Warren Buffet is an example of a generous philanthropist who has pledged to give away all of his multi-billion dollar fortune.

Property is another common type of donation philanthropists make. It is not so simple to give away as money. There is more involved with receiving property, and some charities are not able to accept each type of donation. When it is land or vehicles, a charity will need a purpose for the donation unless they will sell it later to obtain the cash value.

Other forms of property people donate are new or used clothing and items that charity stores known as thrift shops can sell. Even non perishable food items people or organizations give individually or by truckloads count as philanthropic property donations. Individuals or businesses give these to charity center, shelters, or soup kitchens.

Sometimes people overlook the category of services when considering philanthropic activity. Many people need help in various forms. A person might volunteer their time to visit sick people in hospitals or nursing homes, or to help serve or deliver soup kitchen meals. Lawyers and accountants can provide their services to individuals who can not afford them. Teachers can offer to tutor children who need help. Even helping to fix another person's house is a benevolent philanthropic act. Angelina Jolie is a wealthy actress who gives not only money but also her time helping the poor in other countries as an ambassador to humanity for the United Nations.

Gifts from an individual's body are also philanthropic. Donating blood is such an act. This saves injured people's lives and is critical when blood transplants are required. Some individuals will donate a kidney to save another person. Organ donors are those philanthropists who give their bodies' vital components after they die. Their organs can be transplanted to save individuals who will die without them. This makes such donations among the most philanthropic possible.

Philips Curve

Philips Curve is a concept in economics which A.W. Philips created. This curve demonstrates that the relationship between unemployment and inflation is predictable, inverse, and stable. Philips' theory explains that when economies enjoy growth, inflation appears alongside it. This may sound like a negative side effect, but it is not necessarily according to Philips.

The growth coupled with inflation is supposed to create a greater number of jobs and lead to lower unemployment. The idea was generally accepted until the 1970s. At that point, stagflation brought on high unemployment along with inflation. This real world empirical data has at least partially disproven the idea under these circumstances.

The theory that underlies Philips Curve claims that when unemployment changes in an economy, this causes a predictable impact on the inflation of prices. This relationship is said to be inversely related. On the curve, this means that the correlation between unemployment and inflation shows it as a concave (outward) and downward sloping curve. Unemployment is demonstrated on the X axis while inflation is depicted on the Y axis. It pictorially shows how inflation increasing lowers unemployment. The reverse is also shown as higher unemployment reduces inflation.

In the 1960s, economists believed that the result of fiscal stimulus would lead to a higher total demand in the economy. This would case the demand for labor to grow. The total number of workers who were unemployed would diminish, causing firms to increase their wages to be able to competitively vie for the tinier pool of talent. Higher wages would boost costs at corporations. Companies would then choose to pass through these costs to the individual consumers. This would translate to higher prices and finally more inflation as the Philips Curve demonstrates.

Because many governments believed in these ideas, they chose to implement a so called stop-go strategy. They would affect this by establishing a target inflation rate. To attain the desired rate of inflation, they would adapt their monetary and fiscal policies as needed to contract or expand the economy. It no longer worked for them in the 1970s as the once stable and predictable model between unemployment and inflation broke down as stagflation appeared. This caused economists and governments to question the relevance and value of the Philips Curve.

Stagflation happens as economies suffer from poor economic growth at the same time as they have high inflation and more unemployment. Such a case directly contradicts the Philips Curve theories. Until the 1970s, the United States had never suffered from stagflation where such increasing levels of unemployment did not come along with reducing inflation rates.

This is because demand typically falls when economies are stagnant. It makes sense that workers who are unemployed will purchase less. This causes companies to lower their prices to encourage consumer spending. Yet from the years 1973 to 1975, the American economy managed to provide six different contiguous quarters where the GDP declined as inflation tripled. Economists now show that the 1970 occurring minor recession which policymakers aggravated with price and wage controls caused the stagflation to occur.

It was then United States President Richard Nixon who implemented such controls. His imitation of a stop-go strategy caused companies to be confused as to how to react. Because of this, they kept prices elevated more than they would have otherwise. The government no longer employs stop-go strategies since this episode of stagflation. Central banks maintain strict and rigorously enforced inflation targets now so that stagflation is less likely for the future. In the majority of economic circumstances, the Philips Curve is otherwise a true representation of the real world relationship between unemployment and inflation.

Plunge Protection Team (PPT)

The Plunge Protection Team is a nickname given to the President's Working Group on Financial Markets. It came into existence to make economic and financial recommendations on the economy when there are periods of economic chaos. On the team are the heads of the most critical U.S. financial regulatory organizations. This includes the Secretary of the U.S. Treasury, the SEC Securities Exchange Commission Chairman, the Chairman of the Federal Reserve, and the Chairman of the CFTC Commodity Futures Trading Commission.

The Washington Post newspaper created the nick name Plunge Protection Team only a decade later in 1997. President Ronald Reagan originally convened the team as a response to the terrible Black Monday stock market crash. The government was desperate to restore investor confidence in U.S. financial markets. President Reagan called together the group to improve on the efficiency, integrity, and order of them.

The Working Group on Financial Markets was instructed to find out what happened with the financial markets in the U.S. on and around trading day October 19, 1987. They were told to come up with government actions for coordinating efforts and making contingencies to prevent them from happening again when possible.

To carry this out they were told to talk with various representatives from the business world. This included individuals from clearing houses, exchanges, significant market players, and regulating bodies to learn what the market might suggest for non-government solutions.

Finger pointing at first characterized the investigation. The NYSE held the various futures exchanges responsible for the crash. The CME group engaged in a number of studies to refute this by having market experts rationally analyze the events. They refuted the accusations for the problems with these studies.

One positive mechanism came from these initial meetings with the Plunge Protection Team. NYSE and CME group worked to establish circuit breakers between the securities and futures markets. This slowed down or stopped wildly erratic moves in the market. These circuit breakers remain in effect to this day.

The PPT had 60 days from the Executive Order to give this initial report to the President. They were to report from time to time after this as they reached more findings and solutions for recommended changes to the legislation. When the report and finished recommendations were completed, the President did not disband the group as many had expected.

Instead it stayed together to be reconvened on any subsequent crisis and threat to the financial system. This caused some observers to believe that the group had a secret purpose to manipulate markets and ensure they stayed higher. The group covered such issues as the almost collapse of Long Term Capital Management, Terrorism Risk Insurance from September of 2006 and Over the Counter Derivatives Markets and the Commodity Exchange Act in November of 1999.

Most famously the group reconvened during the financial crash of the Great Recession in 2008. In March, 2008 they issued their Policy Statement on Financial Market Developments. It had the PPTs analysis and report on what continued to plague the markets and cause the ongoing market turmoil.

Their final conclusions had to do with the subprime market mortgages. The determined that the main cause of the destructive chain of events started with the rise in delinquencies of these mortgages. They issued another statement on the continuing crisis on October 6 of 2008. In this they announced that the situation in worldwide financial markets continued to be very strained. They assured investors that they were working with global regulators and market participants to take on the problems and restore stability and confidence to markets.

Purchasing Power Parity (PPP)

Purchasing power parity is a method for comparing the various standards of living of different countries and through different times. It also allows economists to compare one nation's economic productivity to another nation's. This economic theory believes that it is possible to compare the various currencies of different countries by analyzing the cost of a basket of goods. The idea states that two currencies are at a fair market value to each other when the basket of goods becomes priced identically in the two countries.

There is a formula for calculating purchasing power parity. It is S= P1/P2. S stands for the exchange rate of a first currency against a second one. P1 is the symbol for the price of goods in the first currency. P2 symbolizes the price of goods in the second currency.

Coming up with a meaningful comparison of goods requires that a considerable range of services and goods should be analyzed. This requires gathering a great amount of information. To help make the process easier, the United Nations worked with the University of Pennsylvania in 1968 to establish the International Comparisons Program.

The purchasing power parity numbers which come from the ICP uses price surveys from around the world which compare and contrast costs for literally hundreds of different goods. These results give international economists the tools they need to create global growth and productivity estimates.

The World Bank compiles a special report on PPP once each three years to compare the nations of the world by both U.S. dollars and their PPP values. Both the OECD Organization for Economic Cooperation and Development and the IMF International Monetary Fund base their recommended policies and economic predictions on the purchasing power parity measurements.

Forex traders have also been known to employ PPP to scout for undervalued and overvalued currencies. Finally investors with foreign corporation stocks or bonds can consider these figures to forecast how exchange rate fluctuations will impact the economy of the country where their investments are based.

When individuals or companies employ PPP, they are utilizing it in place of the market determined exchange rates. This figure provides them with the quantity of currency required to purchase the basket of goods and services used in the equation. This means that inflation rates and cost of living ultimately determine a nation's PPP.

Economists are also able to utilize purchasing power parity to determine which countries have the largest amount of purchasing power. To do this, they take the GDP gross domestic product of countries as a starting point. This is the aggregate dollar amount of every good and service a nation produces in a particular year. The number is among the preferred means of analyzing the economy of a country. Economists can determine this in either market exchange rates or PPP terms.

The PPP measurement will consider the costs of localized services and goods of a given nation as measured in U.S. prices. It contemplates both the inflation rates and the exchange rates in this calculation. The GDP using PPP demonstrates a citizen's purchasing power compared to that of the citizen in another. Since a shirt will usually cost more in one nation than in the other one, purchasing power parity helps to make the calculation fairer. While the 2016 rankings for GDP by market exchange terms show the top five countries as the U.S., China, India, Japan, and Germany, when PPP is used, China ranks ahead of the U.S.

Quantitative Easing

Quantitative easing is the policy where the government purchases bonds and financial instruments by printing money in order to stimulate the economy. Quantitative easing proves to be a monetary policy that the Federal Reserve and other central banks around the world utilize in order to grow the money supply. They do this by boosting the cash reserves in the banking system. This is accomplished via purchasing the government's issued bonds in order to raise their prices.

Since prices and interest rates of bonds move inversely, higher bond prices lead directly to lower long term interest rates. Quantitative easing is commonly employed only after other more traditional means of dominating the supply of money have not worked. These other methods involve lowering discount rates, bank interest rates, and even interbank interest rates to around zero.

Once these traditional means have failed to stimulate the economy, the Fed then steps into the market and directly buys financial instruments. The assets that they purchase include agency debt, government bonds, corporate bonds, and mortgage backed securities, which they purchase from banks and institutions. This entire process is called open market operations. By depositing electronically created money into the banks' accounts, the banks gain additional reserves that permit them to create still additional money from thin air. The Fed hopes that this multiplication of deposits accomplished through the fractional reserve banking system will allow greater amounts of loans to be made to businesses and individuals in order to stimulate the economy.

This quantitative easing policy is not without its risks. It could be too effective or not sufficiently effective, should banks decide to hoard their extra money to boost their capital reserves. This is particularly the case in an environment of rising defaults in the banks' mortgage and other types of loans' holdings.

Recent examples of quantitative easing abound. This subtle form of printing money became more and more common as the financial crisis of 2007 to 2010 grew worse. In these years, the United States engaged heavily in it, tripling the world wide dollar reserves by creating money both at home and abroad. Other Central Banks, such as those of Great Britain and the European Union, similarly engaged in the practice to help mitigate the effects of the crisis and resulting Great Recession. These countries and economic blocks had all already lowered their interest rates to zero or near zero amounts, and they found quantitative easing to be their best remaining option for restarting economic growth.

Real Estate Bubble

A Real Estate bubble occurs as housing prices rise because of increased speculation, actual legitimate demand, and irrational exuberance all working in concert. These bubbles generally begin because of a legitimate rise in demand for housing and Real Estate at the same time as the housing supply is quite limited.

Because of this limit in supplies, it needs quite a significant amount of time in order for the available housing stock to be replenished and grow. In such a climate, speculators appear on the market and begin to really encourage demand. Finally, demand will stagnate and even decrease as the supply is finally increasing to catch up to the prior demand. This results in a catastrophic bursting of the bubble in the form of disorderly, rapid, and sharply decreasing prices that finally become a self-fulfilling prophecy.

In the past, housing markets did not suffer as often from such bubble phenomenon as did other kinds of financial markets like stocks and bonds. This was because the carrying costs and purchasing prices of homes are significant barriers to investment entry for smaller and medium sized investors. Thanks in large part to historically low interest rates and an unfathomable loosening of credit standards, borrowers were able to enter the market in record demand and drive massive orders for houses. Conversely, raising interest rates and tightening up on standards for credit reduces demand effectively, which leads to the Real Estate bubble bursting quickly.

These Real Estate bubbles are also referred to commonly as housing bubbles or property market bubbles. These economic bubbles can inflate either in worldwide real estate markets or only on small local markets. They generally come after the buildup of a land boom. Land booms prove to be the quick growth in market price of houses and land to the point when they attain levels which are ultimately unsustainable and then lead to a sharp decline in said bubble.

The financial crisis and Great Recession of 2007-2009 evolved out of the Real Estate bubble bursting that had inflated from the early 2000s in all major countries of the world. It took years for this bubble to rise as investors abandoned the global stock markets in record numbers following the bursting of the dotcom bubble and resulting 2000 stock market crash. They poured their capital instead into real estate and house properties during the following six years. The craze which surrounded homeownership rose to frightening levels while interest rates were crashing and responsible lending underwriting all but disappeared.

Analysts have estimated as many as 56% of all house purchases in those six years came from individuals who could not have afforded to buy a house under traditional lending requirements. These people became known as the infamous and economy-wrecking subprime borrowers. The overwhelming majority of such loans were issued as adjustable rate mortgages, or ARMs, that carried an upfront lower interest rate with a punishing schedule set to adjust the prevailing interest rate massively upward after from three to five years passed.

The government was much to blame for the irresponsible encouragement of universal homeownership which they pressed banks to allow in those years. Banks responded to the directives by slashing their interest rates and tough requirements. This encouraged a home purchasing bonanza that had not been witnessed in American history heretofore. Prices increased by as much as from 50 percent to 100 percent in various parts of the nation. The bubble sucked in financial speculators who started flipping houses in order to earn even tens of thousands of dollars of profits with only two weeks of holding such properties. Analysts have further estimated after the fact that fully 30 percent of the housing prices were based on purely speculative endeavors from the zenith of the Real Estate bubble in 2005 to 2007.

As the interest rates began to gradually rise while stocks finally rebounded, adjustable rate mortgages started resetting at massively higher interest rates in a show that the economy was beginning to slow down by 2007. Home prices already sat at impossible to justify and sustain levels and the risk premium had finally risen to be too high for the speculators who suddenly ceased buying houses without warning.

Home prices started to plummet after home buyers realized that the prices could in fact drop. This led to an enormous sell off in the associated and now-infamous mortgage backed securities, or MBS market. The home prices finally dropped by over 40 percent in parts of the country that had been the most overheated, like Florida, Nevada, Arizona, Colorado, and California. This led to incredible default rates on mortgages that caused as many as tens of millions of homes to be foreclosed upon by the banks in the following several years.

Recession

A recession is literally defined as the declining of the nation's GDP, or Gross Domestic Product, by a smaller amount than ten percent. This drop in GDP has to occur over greater than a single consecutive quarter in a given year. Gross domestic product stands for the total of all goods and services that a country produces, or the actual total of all business, private, and government spending on the categories of investment, labor, services, and goods.

The terms recession and depression are typically confused and sometimes used interchangeably. They are quite different from each other. Recessions are typically less severe than are depressions. Recessions are generally corrected in significantly less time and with less economic pain for individuals. Depressions furthermore involve drops in GDP of greater than ten percent.

There is no universal consensus on what makes a recession within an economy. Most economists agree on a few different factors that are commonly involved in causing such recessions. Prices might decrease substantially, or alternatively they could go up substantially. The decrease in prices shows that people are spending smaller amounts of money, and this will cause the Gross Domestic Product to go down. Conversely, higher prices can diminish the amounts of public and private spending, similarly causing the Gross Domestic Product to decrease.

As much as governments, individuals, and businesses hate recessions, many economists feel that they are normal for economies to go through, particularly mild ones. They claim that such economic pull backs are a built in part of society and economics. Prices go up and down, and spending and the amount of consumption similarly decreases and increases over time as well. Still, natural decreases in spending are not sufficient to provoke a recession into occurring. Some other factor changes suddenly and leads to sharp spikes or drops in real prices.

For example, the early 2000's recession came about as a result of the dot com industry suddenly and precipitously decreasing in activity. One day, the demand that they had anticipated turned out to be far less than expected. This created enormous failures of companies and significant layoffs that led to production decreases and finally spending cuts. This dot com drop created a shock effect on the gross domestic product, leading to a significant fall in production and output as spending dropped.

The recession had ended by 2003, yet the consequences of it turned out to be dramatic and can still be felt. High paying jobs suddenly disappeared, only to be outsourced to foreign countries. These jobs will likely never return to the United States. Still, as the Gross Domestic Product began growing again, the recession was deemed to have ended. This does not change the fact that numerous individuals still feel the impact of it in their own personal lives.

Similarly, the Great Recession that you saw stem from the financial collapse of 2007-2010 came about as a sudden seizure in the banking industry and credit markets. It has led to the highest levels of real unemployment since the Great Depression, reaching nearly twenty percent when measured by the formula that had been used until President Bill Clinton changed it. Even though this recession has been called over, the unemployment levels have not declined meaningfully. This means that for several more years at least, a great amount of economic pain and hardship will continue to be felt by those countless millions who have lost their jobs in the recession.

Refinancing Boom

A refinancing boom refers to the points in the market where the share of the refinance mortgage applications is greater than 50% of the total applications. This is the definition that home lending agency giant Freddie Mac employs. They determine both the start and the end of ref booms based on this 50% of MBA's survey figure for the weekly applications. This information provides data for both government and nonconforming loans alongside the traditional loans making it a good all inclusive basis.

Under this Freddie definition, the refinancing boom began in 2008 in the third quarter. It lasted almost six years into 2014. This made it the longest lasting refi boom since Freddie Mac began issuing its quarterly report on refinance activity back in 1990. It was actually during the week of May 2nd that the share of refi applications declined under 50%.

The week before this gave a warning that volume would drop below that critical level as total application volume reached its lowest level since December in 2000. Even though refi applications rose above 50% the following week May 9th, this still represented a break in the statistics that Freddie Mac utilizes. This explains why they described the end of the long lasting refi boom in May of 2014.

Because of this it is not easy to concretely define when these refi booms start and finish as the market share of loan volume that is refinancing can fluctuate. Besides this overall mortgage activity volume can be down in total, and yet the market still can be called a refi boom if the refi percentages exceed 50%. This is why there are other competing definitions of what constitutes a refi boom.

Another popular rival definition that has gained some traction on defining refi booms has to do with the volume of overall originations. When the all around origination volume rises on a year over year basis and this happens because of a boom in refinance activity, this better signifies that a refi boom is underway. This can still be somewhat misleading. There could be a seemingly greater number of refinance applications at a given time if home sales are less than impressive. This would lead to a decline in mortgage purchase applications.

Despite these alternative definitions, Freddie Mac continues to use the one it pioneered on refi booms. According to this traditional definition of the booms, Freddie Mac called the end to the longest refinance boom in history during 2014 in the second quarter. This happened in part because the market shifted to one that was dominated by purchases that exceeded 50% of total applications for the first time since the year 2000.

Freddie Mac compiled interesting statistics on this longest refi boom in American history. They saw more than 25 million different American homeowners engage in refinancing their mortgages during the boom. This equated to the total savings in interest payments of more than $70 billion.

A number of industry observers felt that the refi boom actually ended a year earlier than Freddie Mac's official call. Many watchers claimed that cooling of refinance and origination loan activity in 2013 in the spring signaled the end of the refi boom. By that point the market had already taken hits to refinance applications and activity because of the quick increase in the mortgage interest rates.

The higher interest rates removed the incentive for homeowners to continue refinancing their mortgages. This is why many economists called the end of the refi boom a full year before Freddie Mac did.

Roaring Twenties

The 1920s were the original national era of irrational exuberance. In this decade, huge numbers of Americans believed that they could earn enormous fortunes in the stock markets. They ignored the fact that the markets could be volatile. This allowed them to justify investing all of their life savings in stocks. Those who did not have savings were able to get in on the action as well.

They purchased stocks on margin or credit. This worked well until the markets dove on Black Thursday, Black Monday, and Black Tuesday on October 29 of 1929. At this point the country was grossly unprepared for the stock market crash of 1929. The ensuing economic devastation that the crashes caused proved to be a critical element in kick starting the Great Depression.

The conclusion of World War I changed the national mood in the U.S. Americans were jubilant, confident, and optimistic about the future. They saw new inventions appear like radio and the airplane and everything seemed to be possible. The stock market already had earned its reputation for risk by this time. In the 1920s it no longer seemed risky. The country's mood encouraged this as the stock market for once appeared to be an investment in a bright future that could not lose.

With more and more individuals piling into the stock market, prices naturally started going higher. This first became noticeable in 1925. The rest of the year and in 1926 stocks trended higher and lower. In 1927 they put in a strong upward trend and showing. The powerful bull market fed on itself and lured still more individuals to invest in the markets.

A full fledged boom had started by 1928. This resulting boom altered investors' perceptions of the stock market. No one saw this as a place for long term investment at this time. Instead in 1928 the stock market represented a venue in which ordinary Americans felt that they could actually become wealthy quickly.

At this point the enthusiasm for the stock market turned feverish. Everybody all over the country talked about stocks. These discussions over stocks occurred everywhere ranging from barber shops to parties. Newspapers told stories about regular Americans like teacher, maids, and chauffeurs who had made millions of dollars in the markets. This only increased the enthusiasm to invest more.

Not every person could afford to purchase stocks. They solved this problem by allowing regular people to buy stocks on margin. When they could not front enough money to purchase them, their broker would take a 10% to 20% deposit of the price and loan them the additional 80% to 90% to purchase the stocks. This worked well while stocks were rising but in practice was very risky.

When stock prices fell below the amount loaned, brokers would demand that borrowers find the cash to cover the loan immediately in a margin call. Speculators who hoped they could make huge amounts of money in the stock markets ignored this risk and purchased the stocks on margin whenever they could. They felt confident that the practically never ending increase in prices would only continue. They ignored the risks that they were taking.

In early 1929, the race was on across the U.S. to invest in the stock market. Even companies were putting their corporate money into stocks as profits seemed to be a sure thing. Most dangerously, banks began investing customer monies into stocks and did not tell them about it. As long as stocks continue to roar ahead, everything appeared perfect. As the great crash approached in October, these businesses, banks, and speculators had a devastating lesson coming and were caught completely off guard.

Run on the Bank

A run on the bank is the vernacular expression for a bank run. Runs on the banks actually happen as a result of many bank customers deciding to take out their deposits at one time. They do this out of fear that the bank is either broke or on its way to becoming insolvent. When runs on the banks get started, they have a tendency to create their own terrible momentum that leads to a self fulfilling prophecy. The more customers who take out their money, the greater the odds of bank default become, which leads to still more customer deposit withdrawals. If this happens long enough, it will likely upset a bank's finances to the point that the bank encounters bankruptcy as a result.

Runs on the bank can often lead to bank panics. These financial crises result from a large number of banks experiencing bank runs all at once. If the bank panics are not dealt with swiftly and convincingly, then a systemic banking crisis can develop. In such a banking crisis that is system wide, it is not uncommon to witness practically all, or even all, of a country's banking capital disappear.

Once this occurs, numerous bankruptcies follow, many times ending up in a deep and painful economic recession or even depression. Bank runs created a great amount of the economic damage that you saw done in the Great Depression. Associated costs of fixing the mess related to a systemic banking crisis are enormous. Over the last forty years, these expenses around the world have averaged fully thirteen percent of the respective countries' Gross Domestic Products in fiscal costs, leading to losses of economic output that averaged twenty percent of Gross Domestic Product.

Runs on the bank are able to be prevented with a few different strategies. Withdrawals can be suspended. More effectively, deposit insurance systems can be put in place, like the one that the Federal Deposit Insurance Corporation operates in the United States. The Central Bank may also help out banks by performing the function of the lender of last resort in times of banking crises. Such strategies are commonly effective, but not always. Even when countries possess deposit insurance, the bank depositors could still be fearful that they will not have instant access to their bank held deposits while the bank is reorganized by the FDIC.

The reason that runs on the bank are able to happen in the first place is because of the fractional reserve banking system. Modern day banks only keep a small percentage of their demand deposits in cash on hand, typically ten percent in developed nations. The rest of these deposits are tied up in loans that have longer terms than demand deposits. This leads to a mismatch of assets and liabilities. Though some banks keep better reserves than others do, no modern bank keeps sufficient reserves in its vaults to handle the majority of their deposits being withdrawn at a single time.

Secondary Market

The secondary market refers to that securities trading market in which investors are able to purchase and sell securities that they own. Most individuals would simply call this the stock market. It is also true that stocks are additionally sold on the primary market at their first time and point of issue. Secondary markets in the United States include the NASDAQ and NYSE New York Stock Exchange. In Europe they include London's FTSE, the Euro Next, and Germany's Deutsche Bourse.

There are more than simply stocks traded on the secondary market. Stocks do prove to be the most heavily traded securities on these exchanges. Other types of securities available on such markets include bonds and mutual funds. Individual and corporate investors along with investment banks both sell and buy all three types of securities on the secondary markets. Besides this, Freddie Mac and Fannie Mae the GSE government sponsored enterprises buy mortgages on such a secondary market.

These transactions that take place on this secondary market are simply a step away from the original transaction which created the relevant securities in the first place. Looking at an example of this process helps to clarify it. JP Morgan will underwrite mortgages for customers. This actually creates the mortgage which is a security. JP Morgan might then choose to sell the mortgage security on to Freddie Mac in a secondary transaction in this market.

There are important differences between the primary and secondary markets. In the cases where corporations issue their bonds or stocks initially and then sell them directly to various types of investors, this is a primary market transaction. IPOs initial public offerings remain among the best-known and most heavily advertised transactions of the primary market. In such an IPO, the transaction occurs directly between the investment bank IPO underwriter and the buying investor. All resulting proceeds that come from the stock shares would then be delivered to the issuing company directly. The bank would subtract any agreed upon administration costs before handing over the funds.

Later on in the life cycle of these new stock shares, the first investors might opt to sell their individual stakes in the corporation. They would do this on the secondary market. All such transactions occur between investor parties. This means that the resulting proceeds from sales accrue to the investor re-selling the stock. They do not go back to the firm which originally issued the security nor its underwriter investment banks.

In general, prices on the primary market will be pre-arranged in advance of the transaction. Those prices from the secondary market are arranged by the interaction of supply and demand forces. When most investors are convinced that a given stock will rise in value and decide to race out to purchase it, this causes the stock price to rise generally speaking. When investors decide a company is out of favor or it is unable to deliver strong enough earnings results, then the stock price drops as the demand for such a security evaporates.

There are many more secondary markets than just one. The numbers are constantly going up because new financial securities always appear on the markets. Where mortgage assets are concerned, there are a few different secondary markets that exist. This is in part due to the fact that clever investment banks created bundles of mortgages. They then engineered these bundles into securities like MBS and GNMA pools. Finally they resell these to investors on the secondary markets.

The secondary market can also be subdivided further down to two other types of markets. These are the auction market and the dealer market. The auction market is a physical place like a stock market exchange where they bid on and sell securities publicly. The dealer market on the other hand involves purchasing and selling securities via electronic networks which are run over phones, customized order routing machines, or fax machines.

Seven Sisters Oil Companies

Seven Sisters Oil Companies is a phrase that was made famous by Italian state oil Company ENI Chief and Italian businessmen Enrico Mattei back in the 1950s. Mattei used this phrase disparagingly, which he coined in order to refer to the seven Anglo-American oil companies that had formed the "Consortium for Iran" cartel. They became so powerful that they soon dominated the universe of the worldwide petroleum industry in the years from the mid 1940s through the early 1970s.

The group was made up of seven American and British firms Anglo Persian Oil Company (today's British Petroleum), Gulf Oil (most of which became part of British Petroleum and the other parts which joined Chevron), Standard Oil of California or SoCal (today's Chevron), Texaco (later a part of Chevron in a merger), London headquartered Royal Dutch Shell, Standard Oil Company of New Jersey (Esso which became Exxon), and Standard Oil Company of New York or Socony (Mobil, which merged with Exxon to become ExxonMobil).

Before the 1973 oil crisis, the different companies from the Seven Sisters controlled approximately 85 percent of the global oil reserves. Since then, this has shifted dramatically away from the Seven Sisters Oil Companies over to a combination of the OPEC oil cartel nations as well as several state controlled gas and oil companies in the emerging world economies. These include notably Gazprom of Russia, Saudi Aramco of Saudi Arabia, China National Petroleum Corporation, PDVSA/Citgo of Venezuela, National Iranian Oil Company, Petrobras of Brazil, and Petronas of Malaysia.

The Seven Sisters Oil Companies' common history stretches back to the Iranian 1951 nationalization of its foreign dominated oil industry. The Anglo-Iranian Oil Company, which became BP, at this time controlled the Iranian oil industry. Because Iran opted to nationalize its assets and seize the petroleum reserves, the international community placed an embargo on Iran. Once Iran agreed to return to the international oil markets, the State Department of the United States suggested that the oil majors create a major oil companies consortium. Interestingly enough, a few of them were the scions of billionaire oil man John D. Rockefeller and his original American oil monopoly the Standard Oil Company. As a result of the State

Department's appeal, the "Consortium for Iran" arose and saw seven oil majors brought on board the lucrative and influential project.

Anglo Persian Oil Company of the United Kingdom was the original player in Iran and a major player in the Seven Sisters Oil Companies consortium for Iran. The company changed names to the Anglo-Iranian Oil Company before finally becoming British Petroleum. After the company took over the Standard Oil Company of Indiana, which was better known as Amoco, and Gulf branded gas stations, British Petroleum shortened their name to BP back in 2000.

American Gulf Oil was the second company. SoCal acquired much of Gulf in 1984, and this larger firm changed its name to Chevron. Though some of its Gulf service stations in the Northeastern part of the U.S. still bear the Gulf name, the majority of these were bought out in the East coast by either BP or Cumberland Farms.

Royal Dutch Shell of Great Britain and the Netherlands was the third company. American Texaco was the fourth company. They were absorbed by Chevron in 2001. Chevron itself arose from the fifth company in the consortium Standard Oil of California, or the SoCal company of the United States. It changed its name to Chevron in 1984 after acquiring much of Gulf Oil.

The sixth company was American Standard Oil of New Jersey, or Esso. It later changed its name to Exxon before renaming itself Exxon Mobil in 1999 after it acquired the seventh consortium member Mobil. The American company Mobil itself was earlier known as Standard Oil Co. of New York, or Socony.

Interestingly enough, all of these oil companies were either American or British headquartered. ENI, the state oil company of Italy, wished to be a member of the Consortium for Iran, but was turned away by the other members of the Anglo-Saxon controlled Seven Sisters Oil Companies. These seven companies went on to dominate the oil production of the Middle East following the Second World War.

The phrase Seven Sisters Oil Companies became more popular still when British author Anthony Sampson assumed the mantle of the term in his

1975 published book The Seven Sisters. In this work, he unveiled the shadowy world oil cartel that had attempted to crush its competition and to dominate control of the global oil and gas resources.

Because they were well-funded and -organized and operated effectively as an economic cartel, these Seven Sisters managed to exercise great power over the resources, markets, and politics of the Third World oil producers. Yet the power of these seven original oil behemoths became challenged by the rise of OPEC, which was established in 1960. The rise of the all-powerful state owned and run oil companies in many emerging national economies also dealt the Seven Sisters a body blow. Finally, there was a deteriorating global share of both gas and oil reserves held by their home countries of the United States and Great Britain over the years that weakened their home markets in the world oil production arena.

Today only four of the original seven sisters remain, thanks to merger and acquisition activities over the intervening decades. This became necessary for the oil majors to compete against OPEC and the state owned oil companies. The remaining entities are now BP, ExxonMobil, Chevron (Texaco), and Royal Dutch Shell. They are collectively a part of the seven or eight super-major oil companies of the globe also called Big Oil.

Stagflation

Stagflation refers to the simultaneous problems of high unemployment, stagnated economic growth, and persistently high inflation. It is an unlikely scenario, as slowing economies typically reduce demand sufficiently in order to keep higher prices in check. When workers lose their jobs, they purchase less. Businesses are then usually forced to reduce their prices in order to convince remaining customers to buy. It is this typically slower growth in market economies that prevents inflation from running away.

Stagflation policies typically lead to hyperinflation. Central banks that expand the country's money supply as the national supply is restricted do so by printing up additional currency. Monetary policies then create additional credit. This increases demand from consumers. It is the simultaneous supply restrictions that keep companies from producing enough to keep up with the rising demand.

Such a scenario happened in Zimbabwe back in 2004. Their government printed up so much currency that it pushed well beyond stagflation and evolved into ruinous hyperinflation. A stagflation in the United States only transpired in the 1970s. At the time the U.S. government expanded its dollars significantly to try to create additional economic growth. While they did this, President Nixon's wage price controls severely limited business-produced supplies.

The name stagflation actually comes from the 1973 to 1975 era recession. In those six consecutive quarters, the U.S. GDP shrank in size. Inflation literally tripled in 1973 alone, jumping from a relatively tame 3.4% to 9.6%. In the time between February of 1974 and April of 1975, inflation stubbornly remained between 10% and 12%.

Experts today look back at the 1973 Arab-led oil embargo as the crisis that triggered first oil price inflation. At this time, OPEC nations drastically cut their oil exports to the United States, forcing prices to quadruple. The inflation from oil spread to many other parts of the economy dependent on oil and gasoline, such as shipping, rail, and trucking.

The mild recession of 1970 was the precursor to the problems. President Richard Nixon in his bid to be re-elected introduced as series of four fiscal and monetary economic policies that helped to ensure he won. These unfortunately also created the conditions for stagflation a few years later.

Nixon's first mistake was the start of wage and price controls. U.S. businesses were unable to raise their final prices even as import costs were soaring. They could only respond by reducing costs via worker layoffs. That boosted unemployment and further slowed economic growth by lowering demand. Nixon secondly took the U.S. off the gold standard to stop an international run on American gold reserves. This only crushed the value of the dollar and created still higher import prices and yet more inflation.

In order to fight off the inflation, the Federal Reserve had no choice but to continue raising interest rates. These reached their peak of 20% by 1979. Because the Fed did this in an up and down motion, businesses became confused and chose to keep up higher prices.

Though stagflation has not yet reoccurred in the U.S., Americans became worried it might again in 2011. The Fed had begun employing aggressive expansive monetary policies to save the U.S. economy from the grips of the 2008 financial crisis and Great Recession. This caused many to fear that high inflation would return. The economy only grew at low levels form 1% to 2% at this time.

Economists observed stagflation was a viable risk if inflation rose while the economy continued to struggle. Instead, deflation became the serious concern of the day. Massive increases in global liquidity were used to try to fight off this opposite kind of problem.

Standard and Poor's (S&P)

Standard and Poor's is a global ratings agency that is also responsible for the S&P and Dow Jones indices in the stock market. Besides providing ratings on companies and products, they also rate governments' sovereign credit ratings. This company is based in the United States but has 26 offices throughout the globe. The corporation has shortened its name from Standard and Poor's Ratings Services to S&P Global Rating as of April 28, 2016.

The history of Standard and Poor's goes back over 150 years. Today they provide market intelligence that is high quality and well respected. They offer this in the form of their well known credit ratings, global research, and thought leadership. The company operates primarily as S&P Global Market Intelligence and S&P Dow Jones Indices.

Their division S&P Global Market Intelligence proves to be among the world leaders in delivering research and information on a variety of asset classes. They provide this with thought provoking analysis via a number of advanced platforms. Every year the company gathers more than 135 billions individual points of data in the pursuit of this goal. They cover 99% of all the market capitalization in the world. Standard and Poor's wants to be more than just the provider of financial data and intelligence. They are looking to be a creative force for transparency, growth, and the provision of value in the world's capital markets.

Each day this division of the company gathers, scrubs, analyzes, and interprets enormous amounts of data and content. They take this raw information and transform it to intelligence investors can act on covering industries and companies in the worldwide financial markets. Standard and Poor's Global Market Intelligence offers not only data but also valuable insight that helps readers to make more educated and intelligent investment and business decisions that impact the future.

This division boasts several core beliefs. These are relevance, accuracy, timeliness, and completeness. The group proves to be a foremost purveyor of analytics, news, research, and information to a variety of groups around the globe. Beneficiaries of this information include corporations, government agencies, universities, and professionals.

The solutions and data which lead the industry come from their subsidiaries SNL Financial and S&P Capital IQ. These combine to put together data from individual sectors and the comprehensive market with news and analytics. The tools that result allow the group's clients to perform a wide variety of functions. They can track their performance, identify ideas for investments, generate alpha, grasp dynamics of the competition in an industry, determine credit risks, and produce valuations.

This division boasts over 10,000 employees operating in 20 countries around the globe.

The other principal division of Standard and Poor's is the S&P Dow Jones Indices. This group turns out to be the biggest international source for concepts, research, and data on indices. It counts among its legendary financial indicators the Dow Jones Industrial Average and the S&P 500 indices. It has been working with these indicators for more than 120 years to create forward thinking market solutions which help to meet needs of both retail and institutional investors.

They began with launching the Dow Jones Industrial Average in 1896 and later produced the S&P 500 in 1957. This has made them an engine in many of the most critical financial creations of the 20th century. They now offer in excess of 1 million different indices that run the spectrum of many different asset classes throughout the world. The company claims that more assets have been invested in different products that are based on their indices than with any other company on earth.

Sub-prime Mortgage Crisis

The sub-prime mortgage crisis proves to be a still going financial and real estate crisis. It continues to revolve around the steep decline that you saw in American housing prices, the resulting increase in numbers of mortgage delinquencies and finally foreclosures, and the ultimate fall of securities that are backed up by these sub-prime mortgages.

The problems began with the fact that around eighty percent of all United States mortgages that banks gave out to sub-prime borrowers, or people with less than perfect credit, turned out to be adjustable rate types of mortgages. Housing prices actually reached their highest point in the middle of 2006 and then began sharply falling. This caused refinancing of interest rates on mortgages to be harder to obtain. The double edged sword of adjustable rate mortgages resetting at their higher rates started, causing an enormous number of delinquencies and finally foreclosures in mortgages.

The greater problem came as these mortgages underlay a number of financial securities that many financial firms held in huge numbers. They saw most of their value disappear in the following months. Investors around the world then began to dramatically cut back on the quantities of collateralized debt obligations and other mortgage securities that they bought. Besides the damage that increasing sub-prime mortgage delinquencies and foreclosures created themselves and for the investments based on them, this sub-prime mortgage crisis led to a fall in the ability of the banking system to engage in lending. This caused significantly tighter credit and lower rates of growth throughout the developed world, in particular in Europe and the United States,that are still plaguing the industrial countries.

Ultimately, the sub-prime mortgage crisis arose as a result of easy up front loan terms which banks made to borrowers. Both the borrowers and the banks felt confident that the loans could be easily refinanced into better terms as needed, since housing prices were steadily rising over a long term trend. Financial incentives were provided to sub-prime mortgage originators.

This coupled, with fraud that borrowers and lenders engaged in, significantly boosted the quantities of sub-prime mortgages to customers who should have received standard conforming loans or who should not have received loans at all. When the easy interest rate terms expired, the majority of sub-prime loan holding consumers could not refinance at the better rates in which they had believed. The interest rates reset higher, dramatically increasing the monthly mortgage payments.

Home prices started falling to the point that homes were no longer even worth as much as the original mortgage, meaning that they could not be sold to pay off the mortgage obligation. Instead, the borrowers' best interest lay in going through foreclosure and walking away from the hopelessly underwater homes. This continuous epidemic of foreclosures that began with the sub-prime mortgage crisis is still a major continuous part of the world wide financial and economic crisis. The foreclosures are still taking away wealth from consumers and sapping away at the damaged banks' balance sheets.

Too Big To Fail

Too Big To Fail refers to the disturbing but proven concept that some businesses have become so enormous and systemically important that the jurisdictional government has no choice but to save them from failing with whatever means necessary. The governments feel they must deliver material assistance to the firms in order to prevent a catastrophic rogue wave effect from reverberating across the entire economy.

The simple explanation for how a company can be so important to an entire economy is this. When such an enormous firm fails, all of the companies that count on it for parts of their revenue can also be compromised and fail, as well as its debt holders and ancillary services providing companies that work with the failing massive firm. Jobs then become eliminated en masse. For this reason, the expenses involved with a simple bailout or government backed guarantees of the mega corporation are significantly less than the cost of overall widespread economic failures. It explains why governments will often opt for the bailout as the less expensive answer to the moral problem.

Too Big To Fail especially pertains to commercial banks and financial services firms. These financial companies are so critical for the United States' and other Western economies that it would create havoc and spread financial ruin if they declared bankruptcy. Because of this, the American and British governments especially opted in the Global Financial Crisis of 2008-2009 to spare the banks and other financial service firms.

They saved the bank creditors and holders of counter party risk. As an unwished for side effect, they allowed the managers and company board members to keep their enormous salaries and incredible bonuses. Throughout the last years of the 2000's, the United States' Federal Government doled out approximately $700 billion in order to shore up such critical failing corporations as Bear Stearns, AIG, and the major banks which stood on the edge of financial ruin.

It was investors' total evaporation in confidence of the major financial institutions that led to their near-downfall back in the years 2008 and 2009. Especially the investment banks ran into trouble as they had become unbelievably leveraged (to the tune of from forty to one and eighty to one) when suddenly their mortgage loan-based assets and derivatives plunged in value as the subprime mortgage crisis spiraled out of control. Both stake holders and creditors quickly began to have doubts in their financial solvency as their balance sheets crumbled.

The defining moment in the Too Big To Fail crisis erupted when the government did not step in to prevent Lehman Brothers investment bank from failing. This has become widely known as the "Lehman moment." As widespread chaos erupted in the financial markets, regulators suddenly became painfully aware that these largest companies were so intricately connected that it would take enormous financial bailouts in order to stop literally half of the U.S. financial sector from collapsing.

Once the bailouts had intervened to save the major Too Big To Fail investment banks, only two remained standing. Even the survivors Morgan Stanley and Goldman Sachs were both forced to convert to traditional commercial banks so that they could be backstopped by the FDIC. Bear Stearns was effectively wound down, Lehman's skeleton was bought out by Barclays of Great Britain, and once-mighty Merrill Lynch became a subsidiary of Bank of America. The shadow banking industry had all but disappeared overnight.

The government then attempted to address the issues of Too Big To Fail financial firms. The U.S. Congress passed the Dodd-Frank Wall Street Reform and Consumer Protection Act of 2010. The idea was to create restrictions which would make it far more difficult for such conditions to flourish again. They hoped to sidestep having to extend other bailouts in the future.

The Act made the financial institutions create forms of "living wills" so that their plans are in place in order to rapidly liquidate assets if they have to file for bankruptcy. An internationally based consortium of financial regulators came up with a new set of rules in November of 2015 to force the major global banks to raise their capital by $1.2 trillion more in additional debt funding which they are able to convert into equity or write off if they suffer catastrophic losses again.

Total Public Debt

Total public debt refers to all of the national debt which the United States owes to its various creditors and other agencies within the government to whom it owes money. This amount grows in years where there are deficits as the government spends more funds than it receives in taxes.

The aggregate national debt shrinks in surplus years as the federal government receives a greater amount of money that it spends. Every year of the Obama administration has been a deficit year that increased the debt. As of the end of Fiscal 2016, the government's total public debt amounted to $19.7 trillion.

The total public debt includes all money owed to Americans and foreigners as well as other agencies within the government. As such, the gross national debt for the country is made up of two components. The first of these is marketable debt which the public and foreign countries hold. This includes instruments such as Treasury bills, bonds, and notes.

Investors regularly buy and sell this debt on the bond markets. Any investor who is not a part of the federal government is considered to be a part of this class of debt. This means T bills held by consumers, companies, banks and financial institutions, the Federal Reserve, and local, state, and foreign governments are all included in this category of debt. As of July 29, 2016 this portion of the debt amounted to $14 trillion.

The other category of the total public debt is the debt which other government accounts hold. This is also called intra-governmental debt. These debts are also comprised of Treasuries, only these can not be bought and sold. This category of debt is like IOUs kept in federal government administered accounts. The country owes it to beneficiaries of programs, as with the Social Security Trust Fund or the Medicare Trust Fund. These government accounts once had surpluses and invested them over time in Treasury securities. The amount which they are owed includes principal plus interest earnings. On July 29, 2016, this category of the total public debt equaled $5.4 trillion.

Together, the two categories which make up the total public debt equaled $19.4 trillion on the July 29, 2016 date. This represented fully 106% of the prior twelve month national GDP for the United States. Foreigners held $6.2 trillion worth of the debt at this point equivalent to about 45% of the debt which the public held or 32% of the aggregate public debt. The largest foreign holders proved to be China and Japan. As of May 2016, China owned about $1.25 trillion while Japan held $1.15 trillion worth of U.S. government debt.

Usually, the government's debt goes up as and when the government spends monies on entitlements, interest on the debt, and budgetary programs. It similarly decreases as taxes and other monetary receipts accrue. Both categories change throughout the months of the fiscal year.

The government does not in practice issue Treasury debt itself on a day by day basis as it spends money. Instead, this is issued or redeemed according to the government's money management operations. The total amount of money which Treasury is authorized to borrow is restricted by the debt ceiling of the United States. Congress conveniently lifts this every time the ceiling is hit.

Trans Pacific Partnership (TPP)

The Trans Pacific Partnership TPP represents a trade agreement that has been put together by twelve countries with borders on the Pacific Rim. Participants signed the final version of the deal in Auckland, New Zealand on February 4, 2016. This signing culminated the end of seven long years of negotiating the treaty. In order to enter into effect, the treaty must be ratified by the member states' legislatures. This includes the U.S. Congress, where opposition to the treaty has been intense and bipartisan from many members of both parties.

There are 30 different chapters to the Trans Pacific Partnership. Their goal is to encourage job creation and retention, economic growth, innovation, higher living standards, competitiveness and productivity, poverty reduction, better government and transparency, and better protection of the environment and labor. This TPP is made up of agreements that reduce tariff and non tariff barriers to trade. It also creates a means of resolving disputes through investor state settlement.

Originally the Trans Pacific Partnership was born from the Trans Pacific Strategic Economic Partnership Agreement that Singapore, New Zealand, Chile, and Brunei signed back in 2005. Starting in 2008, other nations on the Pacific Rim began to discuss a wider arrangement. This included The United States, Vietnam, Peru, Mexico, Malaysia, Japan, Canada, and Australia. This increased the nations who were a part of the trade negotiations to 12 countries.

Previously in force trade agreements of the countries participating will be amended to not conflict with the TPP. Deals that offer better free trade will still be in effect. The Obama administration looks at the TPP as a pair of treaties. Its twin is the still under discussion TTIP Transatlantic Trade and Investment Partnership between the European Union and the United States. The two deals are generally similar.

The original goal of the talks was to conclude negotiations in the year 2012. The final deal stretched on for another three years because of conflicts over difficult issues like intellectual property, agriculture, investments, and services. The 12 nations at last came to an agreement on October 5, 2015. The U.S. Obama administration has made implementing this TPP one of its principle goals for trade. On November 5, 2015, President Obama announced to Congress he would sign the deal and released a public version of the treaty for any interested American individuals and organizations to review. The U.S. President along with the other 11 leaders all signed the TPP February 4, 2016.

In order for the Trans Pacific Partnership to take effect, all of the signors have to ratify it within two years. In case it is not completely ratified by all parties in advance of the February 4, 2018 deadline, there is an alternative arrangement. It will become effective after minimally 6 signing countries with a combined GDP of greater than 85% of all the signing countries ratify it. This means that the U.S. must ratify if for it to ever take effect.

Other countries may be able to join the trade block in the future. Countries that have shown an interest in joining include South Korea, India, Bangladesh, Cambodia, Indonesia, Laos, Thailand, Colombia, the Philippines, and Taiwan. South Korea did not get involved with the original 2006 agreement. The U.S. invited it to join after South Korea and America concluded their own free trade agreements. South Korea is likely to be the first country to join in a next wave expansion of the group. First it will have to work through TPP treaty issues in agriculture and vehicle manufacturing.

Transatlantic Trade Investment Partnership (TTIP)

The Transatlantic Trade and Investment partnership represents a U.S. and European agreement for mutual trade and investment. In essence it is a free trade deal that the two economic superpowers are working to ratify. The two parties began the initiative in the June of 2013 G8 meeting. U.S. President Obama, European Commission President Barroso, and European Union Council President Van Rompuy introduced the idea and began working on the project.

The goal of the TTIP is to encourage both trade and investment. Governments on both sides believe that this will result in more economic growth and jobs for citizens of both sides of the Atlantic Ocean. Negotiations have been complex and mostly held in secret. The U.S. side is headed by the USTR, or Office of the United States Trade Representative. The Europeans are led by the European Commission. This EC handles negotiations for all 28 EU member countries.

TTIP turns out to be the largest and grandest vision for a trade agreement that has ever been attempted. This is because the United States and European Union economic blocks make up nearly fifty percent of the GDP of the entire world. The impacts on trade are expected to be substantial. Small to medium sized enterprises will gain several benefits in access to the new markets. They will have other countries to which they can export. They will also gain the ability to import input materials from other countries. It is anticipated they will have the ability to gain investments in their businesses at a cheaper, better price as well.

Consumers are supposed to benefit also. Lower prices are expected in both economic blocks because of the reduced tariffs and increased competition. This will improve the purchasing power of residents on both sides of the Atlantic and also help to create more jobs.

Twenty-four different chapters comprise the actual Transatlantic Trade and Investment Partnership. These have been divided into three principal topics. The topics are Market Access, Rules, and Regulatory Cooperation.

Market Access pertains to opening up markets. The goal is to allow for improved competition. Besides this, the architects of the agreement are trying to make it easier for products to flow back and forth across the Atlantic.

The rules section has to do with trade and investment. This area's goal is to increase the fairness and ease of importing, exporting, and investing for American businesses in Europe and European businesses in America. Rules cover a number of different important concepts. These include Energy and Raw Materials, Sustainable Development, Small and Medium Sized Enterprises, Customs and Trade Facilitation, Competition, Investment Protection, Geographical Indications, Intellectual Property, and the Government to Government Dispute Settlements.

The area of Regulatory Cooperation pertains to important regulation differences between the United States and the European Union. Both groups often have the same quality and safety levels that they insist on from specific goods. The problem is that each side employs its own procedures in considering the identical product. This imposes high costs on companies who produce the items. It can be prohibitively expensive for smaller to medium sized businesses.

There have been a number of objections raised by protestors to this free trade agreement, particularly in Europe. Many individuals on both sides of the Atlantic oppose the secrecy that surrounds the negotiations. The protesters have concerns that interest groups are creating special rules for larger companies.

The European labor markets are worried that their working conditions and benefits will suffer. Environmental groups are all concerned that environmental standards and safeties that are higher in Europe will be watered down as a result of the free trade initiative.

U.S. Dollar

The U.S. Dollar refers to the official currency of the United States. This is also the world's largest reserve currency since the end of the Second World War when the American economy was the only one still standing at full productive capacity after the ravaging destruction of the global war left most of Europe and Asia in economic ruin.

The U.S. Dollar value is measurable by three different means. These are exchange rates, foreign exchange reserves, and Treasury notes. The most commonly utilized means of valuing the dollar is by looking at exchange rates. It is important to understand all three measures to know where the future value of the global reserve currency the dollar is headed.

The dollar value has benefited from all three of these metrics of its worth rising since the year 2011. There are several key reasons that explain this. On the one hand, when any worldwide crisis erupts, the dollar becomes the preferred safe haven global primary reserve currency. It is mostly because skittish investors run to the U.S. Treasuries instruments which they perceive to be the safest liquid investments in the world. Despite the fact that this is no longer in fact the best-rated or safest debt in the world, nevertheless investors still run to it according to their longstanding habits since the end of World War II.

Another reason the dollar measurements have continued to gain is because its only real rival in the world (the euro and) the European Union has not been successful at increasing the economic growth even with massive runaway quantitative easing programs. Investors worried in 2012 about the Greek-started Sovereign Debt Crisis in Europe. Both of these problems have discouraged demand for the EU's euro. It is still a growing second choice as a global currency though.

The Chinese currency the Yuan has not been able to gain much traction as an alternative currency to the dollar because of the slowdown in economic growth there that began in 2015. Both China and fellow Asian economic superpower Japan continuously artificially deflate the values of their currencies by buying dollars. This allows them to make their exports cheaper overseas which is good for their respective economic growth rates.

Finally, there is a perception that U.S. interest rates which the Federal Reserve sets are going to slowly continue increasing while the interest rates in Europe continue to decline. Yet the dollar was not always so strong, nor is its future strength assured. The current strengthening period from 2011 actually reversed the long-term dollar decline that started back in the year 2002.

Three critical pressures all still exist and have not been adequately addressed. In fact they are actually getting worse by the year. This will finally cause the dollar's longer-term decline to resume over the medium to long range time frame. The biggest drag on the U.S. Dollar is the fact that the American Federal debt now exceeds an eye watering $20 trillion. The foreign debt holders have long been concerned that the Federal Reserve will simply deflate away the value of the dollar so that it will be cheaper to pay back debts that cost less in their own declining dollar currency. Because of this, long-term largest U.S. debt buyers Japan and China have reduced their Treasury purchases in an alarming and worrisome sign of the times.

The long-lasting quantitative easing program of the U.S. in the Global Financial Crisis and Great Recession caused the Federal Government to monetize the debt. This strengthened the dollar and ensured lower interest rates. This is now coming to an end, and investors fear a resume in the dollar's longer-term decline.

Secondly, because of this massive and growing toxic debt bomb, there is also enormous pressure on both Congress and the American President to reduce spending or increase taxes in the U.S. Either of these actions will impact economic growth in the U.S. negatively.

Finally, as foreign investors like Japan and China have more choices of viable foreign reserve currencies today than ever before, they are naturally prudently diversifying their reserve currency portfolios and investments into non dollar denominated investments and assets. It all spells long-term terminal decline for the U.S. Dollar.

Unique Selling Proposition (USP)

A Unique Selling Proposition, or USP, refers to the slogan or idea that sets apart the particular company's products, goods, and services from their main business competition. It is typically expressed by a single, often short, sentence which succinctly sums up the point and purpose of the company's primary line of business. Another way of putting this is that the USP acts as the overriding theme of a firm's marketing plan and endeavors. Ultimately, this proposition strives to answer the customers' query of why they should purchase a given company's products instead of their competitors' goods.

It is critical that the Unique Selling Proposition offers customers and possible customers alike a precise and well-defined benefit which appeals to them directly. This means that the USP can not simply describe better service or that which offers more value. Instead, the proposition should answer two questions directly. The first is what will set apart a service or product from those the competition offers? The second is what can the product offer that consumers determine to be worthwhile or worthy of spending their money on it?

Small businesses in particular find the Unique Selling Proposition critical for their ongoing operations. This is because they must compete against both larger retail corporations as well as other smaller businesses like themselves. It does not matter how superior a given product or service may be if consumers are not aware of its value and do not see a viable reason to purchase it over those which the competition offers them.

The history of the Unique Selling Proposition dates back to the middle years of the twentieth century. It was then that Rosser Reeves developed the concept. He was an American advertising executive who operated in the depression, Second World War, and post world war eras of the United States. Reeves held a personal conviction about the point of advertising. He felt that its only reason for being lay in conveying the specific slogan of a firm which got across their service or product message effectively.

He fiercely believed that such a slogan should never be changed. Among his best known USPs Reeves developed was one for candy maker Mars/M&M's. This M&M's candy slogan so memorably claimed, "The milk chocolate melts in your mouth, not in your hands."

There have been countless effective other Unique Selling Propositions throughout modern marketing history. Some of the most effective are the ones consumers never forget. Hallmark Corporation's USP is "When you care enough to send the very best." Subway sandwiches are memorably referred to as "Subs with under six grams of fat." The Men's Warehouse has its, "You're going to like the way you look – I guarantee it." FedEx Corporation claims effectively, "When it absolutely, positively has to get there overnight."

Some Unique Selling Propositions became so well remembered that they are even remembered years after a company chooses to abandon them for some reason. Wendy's Hamburger chain, Taco Bell, and Dr. Pepper represent three classic examples of companies which had a USP that embodied this multi-generational slogan appeal. Wendy's famously asked Americans, "Where's the beef?" for years before finally moving on with other far less memorable selling propositions. Taco Bell's little Chihuahua Dinky emphatically claimed, "Yo quiero taco bell!" and "Bless you, Taco Bell" for literally years. Dr. Pepper /7 Up Corporation famously reminded Americans for many decades that their flagship American iconic soft drink Dr. Pepper really is "Just what the Dr. ordered."

According to the strict insistence of USP creator Rosser Reeves, all of these companies broke his cardinal rule of changing slogans which were wildly successful. Many of them paid the price in their subsequent decline in business brand appeal and resulting falling sales and profits.

Universal Basic Income (UBI)

Universal basic income (UBI) is known by a variety of names in different countries and continents. Among the more popular are basic income, citizen's income, unconditional basic income, basic income guarantee, universal demo grant, and UBI. This represents a type of social security welfare program and safety net. In it, all residents or citizens of a nation periodically receive an amount of money which the government or another public institution gives them unconditionally. They receive this on top of and regardless of any other income they earn from work or investment returns. When the money is given out to any persons who live with less than the government-mandated poverty line, it is also known as partial basic income.

This universal basic income and its distribution systems could be financed by the revenues and turnover of publically owned enterprises. These are many times referred to as a citizen's dividend or a social dividend. Such a strategy is a component of a market socialism model, as opposed to market capitalism in which participants' incomes are based on their abilities, hard work, and opportunities. Taxation is another means of paying for such basic income schemes.

It was Thomas Paine's *Agrarian Justice* published in 1795 where he wrote about capital grants to be provided at the age of majority that began the debates concerning universal basic income within the United States. Up through the year 1986, the phrase which referred to this basic income concept most commonly was "social dividend." After that year, the universal basic income wording gained universal appeal. There are many well-known proponents of the social and economic philosophy. Among them are Ailsa McKay, Philippe Van Parijs, Hillel Steiner, Andre Gorz, Guy Standing, and Peter Vallentyne.

In the United States, this Universal Basic Income has been discussed on a number of different occasions as a serious idea for public policy. The numbers which have been bandied about for Americans amount to approximately $1,000 per month, which would be sent via check to every American. Among the conservatives who espoused the concept and argued for it to be implemented were legendary Nobel prize-winning economist Milton Friedman and former Republican President Richard Nixon.

The base case for this Universal Basic Income has been most effectively argued and written extensively about by Andy Stern, who was once the Service Employees International Union president and who serves as a Columbia University professor since then. He published a book called *Raising the Floor* in which he argued dramatically and effectively for the UBI.

Stern argues that the concept of a basic guaranteed income has become more necessary for two reasons. On the one hand, the wars on poverty programs have not been so effective nationally. On the other, the rapid advance of technology has led to unparalleled job dislocation and disruption for millions of American workers. This program would deliver an effective floor, or social safety net, to every American.

Critics of the plan in the U.S. have asked how the Federal Government would possibly afford to pay for this proposed program. Stern referenced the 126 existing separate government programs which each already distribute money to American citizens. Some of these might be rolled into the Universal Basic Income program. Besides this, additional taxes would have to be introduced in order to make the proposal a reality. Economists have predicted that implementing such a UBI would require around $3 trillion each year in funding.

Despite the fact that this concept has many critics, it is also possibly the only significant ideology in the early twenty-first century which has supporters on both the right and the left sides of the political, economic, and social spectrum.

The Swiss were given a vote on the UBI issue for their own country in the late spring of 2016, and they soundly rejected it. Interestingly though, the same voters answered an exit poll claiming they expected to see this policy implemented in Switzerland within the next 25 years.

Velocity of Money

The velocity of money proves to be the speed at which money is changing hands. When the velocity of money is higher, then money is rapidly going from one hand to the next. This allows for a comparatively smaller amount of the money supply to cover a significant number of purchases. Conversely, if the velocity of money turns out to be lower, then the money is going from one hand to the next at a slower rate. This requires a greater supply of money to cover the same quantity of purchases.

The velocity of money is never the same. Such velocity will change along with the preferences of consumers. Besides this, it goes up and down as prices or money's real value fall or rise. Should the real value of money prove to be lower, then the levels of prices are higher. A greater quantity of bills would have to be utilized to pay for purchases. Assuming that money supply is constant, velocity of money has to go up to be able to pay for all purchases. The velocity of money also shifts as the Fed changes the money supply. These changes might cause price levels and money's value to stay the same.

The velocity of money turns out to be the single most critical factor in determining the impacts of any changes to the money supply. As an example, pretend that you buy a piece of pizza. The waiter takes the money that he is paid from this transaction and employs it to pay for dry cleaning. The dry cleaner owner next uses the money to wash his car. This goes on again and again until finally the bill is removed from circulation. Since bills can stay in circulation for literally decades, one bill will generally allow for a vast number of multiples of its face value to be transacted along the way.

The equation that demonstrates how velocity of money relates to the money supply, output, and the price level is expressed as M times V equals P times Y. In this equation, M represents the money supply and V stands for velocity, while P represents the price level and Y is the amount of output. Since P times Y yields the country's Gross Domestic Product, you could also say that V equals GDP over M, or velocity is Gross Domestic Product over money supply. In practice, the equation tells you that a certain Gross Domestic Product level that contains a tinier money supply will require a higher velocity of money so that all purchases can be funded. This means that velocity will go up in this scenario.

Velocity of money equations can also be altered to give percent changes in velocity of money equations. With velocity of money equations, you might employ them to measure the impact that any changes in the velocity, money supply, and price level have on one another. Only the output, represented by Y, would be fixed in such changes, since quantity of output does not change in short time frames.

Voodoo Economics (Reaganomics)

Voodoo Economics is also known as Reaganomics. The term was originally used by President George H.W. Bush (Bush the Elder) to refer disparagingly to the economic policies of his predecessor President Ronald Regan. Ironically President Bush served for eight years as the vice president under Ronald Regan after he made those remarks.

Before eventual President George H.W. Bush served as the VP of President Reagan, he considered his one-day running mate's economic policies the Voodoo Economics as unorthodox and ineffectual. This was because Ronald Reagan loved supply-side economics, wanted to cut back taxes on corporate and personal income, and planned to restrict taxes on capital gains.

The more popular term for the so-called Voodoo Economics changed into Reaganomics over time as these economic policies became wildly successful. The policies of the United States' fortieth president who served from 1981 to 1989 were considered experimental at the time. President Reagan suggested that the economy (which was under a terrible recession since the time of President Jimmy Carter) could be massively stimulated by unconventional methods. These would eventually include massive and across the board tax cuts, significantly lowered social spending, greatly increased spending on the military, and the financial deregulation of American markets. President Reagan introduced these measures to combat the lengthy era of economic and financial stagflation which had started back under President Gerald Ford in the year 1976.

While pre-Vice President George Bush the Elder intended for the term Voodoo Economics to be negative and harmful, the later adopted phrase Reaganomics served both critics and proponents of the policies of President Reagan. This set of policies came from the ideas of trickle down economics theory. Such an idea believed that by decreasing taxes, particularly those on companies, the government could stimulate the economy and increase economic growth. The concept held that as corporations found their expenses were reduced by federal policies, these savings would eventually find their way on down into the remainder of the national economy. This would then cause a boost in the growth rate.

As part of his plan, President Reagan unleashed a four part strategy to lower inflation and to increase the job and economic growth. He started by cutting back the federal government's spending on programs which were domestically based. Next he cut taxes for especially businesses, but also on individual investments and personal tax rates. Third, he decreased the burdensome regulations that handcuffed corporations and companies. Finally, he fostered a lower growth rate of money within the U.S. economy.

While President Reagan did manage to lower the domestic program spending, he over compensated for it with his boost to military spending. This caused a financial net deficit and grew the U.S. debt burden during both of his four year terms. He did effectively slash the highest individual income tax rate down from an eye watering 70 percent to 28 percent. Corporate tax top rates declined from 48 percent down to 34 percent.

Reagan moved on by cutting through all of the restrictive economic regulations which President Jimmy Carter had enacted. He also finally put an end to the dreaded and stifling price controls which still remained on natural gas and oil, cable television, and long distance phone service. During his second term, President Reagan encouraged a Federal monetary policy which helped to finally stabilize the American dollar versus major foreign currencies.

Towards the close of the second term of President Reagan, he had increased the Federal government's tax revenue base from $517 billion of his incoming year 1980 to $909 billion by his final year of 1988, effectively almost doubling it. He had cut inflation back to four percent, and he had pushed down the unemployment rate to under six percent. Economists and politicians may continue to spar regarding the ultimate impacts of the Reaganomics/ Voodoo Economics, yet no one argues that it did bring on what has become among the strongest and longest lasting eras of continuous prosperity in the history of the United States. From the years 1982 to 2000, the DJIA Down Jones Industrial Average increased in level by almost 14 times. The economy increased the job base by 40 million new ones during those heady years.

Welfare

Welfare is a social program that the government uses to attempt to provide for its citizens' well being. This could happen with social security, social welfare programs, or even government sponsored financial aid. Corporate welfare is generally described as the government directly supporting companies instead of permitting the free market to close down inefficient businesses. Governments that grow their welfare programs excessively find that they are called welfare states.

Any type of program that has the government giving services or money directly to citizens in need of help can be called welfare. This means that lots of government programs are forms of welfare, even when the citizens and critics do not realize it. Still others say that still more welfare programs are needed to adequately take care of people's needs.

Social welfare provisions are what the majority of people are describing when they talk about it. These programs offer minimum income standards to those who have lost their jobs, are old, or are disabled. The government feels an ethical obligation to help these individuals who could not live without help. By allowing them a chance to find work again, the government ultimately helps out the economy and nation as a whole.

As an example, those who have lost their jobs can get welfare assistance in the form of unemployment as they are seeking replacement work. This is offered as cash assistance and sometimes as food stamps. If you become disabled and can no longer work, then you are able to obtain the same type of help, even though you do not have to look for work to be eligible.

A great number of countries today feature national health care programs. These prove to be enormous welfare systems. In these systems, every group in the country is able to access medical care when they need help. The U.S. does not yet have a functioning universal health care system set up, though one has been passed by congress and President Obama for the future.

A free universal welfare system that runs throughout the U.S. is free schooling until the end of high school. The government pays for all associated costs, even food and transportation when it is required. Because most critics do not consider free public education to be welfare, there is little controversy surrounding it.

World Currency

A world currency refers to the idea of there being a single monetary unit that is accepted the world over by all nations, businesses, and peoples. As of 2017 (and probably for the foreseeable future), there is no true world currency. There have been many ideas put forward for a single currency over the last few decades. Among these are the International Monetary Fund's SDR Special Drawing Rights and the world's most popular crypto-currency Bitcoin. Yet despite these creative ideas which do show promise for the medium to longer term future, the only contender for title holder of world currency today is the United States dollar.

The U.S. dollar became the dominant reserve currency of the world, the closest thing to a world currency, following the Second World War. This transpired for two reasons. At the end of World War II, most of the economies of the European continental nations, including Great Britain's, were largely devastated. The U.S. economy was the only one left standing intact and as such was the largest in the world at that point. The second reason was that the U.S. had by then amassed the largest gold stocks in the world. This was an era where gold still backed global currencies and proved which currencies were the strongest.

For several decades, the U.S. remained the largest unchallenged economy, and so dollars naturally backed by gold were treated as good as gold. This was still the case even after the U.S. abandoned the gold standard in favor of printing limitless quantities of dollars to finance the growth of the world economy ostensibly. The break with the gold standard did substantially weaken the dollar's position. As a result of this, President Richard Nixon-orchestrated event from 1972, several other world currency challengers gradually arose to threaten the dollar's global dominance.

These were the euro and the Japanese yen. Thanks to their steady development, they have become regional settlement currencies used in European spheres and increasingly in Asian trade, respectively. It is true the American dollar is still the biggest reserve currency in the globe. Yet it has significantly depreciated (versus gold especially) in the last forty-five years since the country chose to abandon the Breton Woods Agreement at the same time as the euro and yen have grown. In fact it is no accident that the three largest economies or economic blocks also boast the three most powerful currencies which dominate the three spheres of the world economy (Americas, Europe, and Asia).

The world currency situation has further shifted away from exclusive settlement in U.S. dollars because of the growth and multiplication of Forex cross currency pairs. New currency pairs such as AUD/JPY (Australian dollars versus Japanese yen) make it possible for direct currency trade and settlement without American dollars having to be involved.

With 185 currencies in the world today, there is no doubt that the dollar remains the most heavily utilized across the globe. As for the other 184 national currencies, the majority of these are only employed within their own national boundaries. While it is true that any of these could in theory take over the role of world currency from the dollar, it is also unlikely that any of them will for some time.

There are several reasons why this is the case. The main one is that the U.S. dollar remains the most powerful world currency. It is not just the domineering size of the U.S. economy as compared to its rivals. Fully more than a third of all the world's economic output derives from nations which either use the dollar or have pegged their own national currencies to the value of the dollar. This results from not only the seven countries which have adopted the U.S. dollar, but another 89 nations that maintain their own national currencies within a tight trading range against the value of the dollar.

Another statistic that underpins the dollar is the fact that over 85 percent of all Forex trading and transactions are connected with the American dollar. Add to this the fact that 39 percent of all debt in the world is dollar currency-issued, and it becomes clear why so many foreign banks require huge amounts of dollars to conduct business operations. This is true even in their own home markets overseas.

www.ingramcontent.com/pod-product-compliance
Lightning Source LLC
Chambersburg PA
CBHW051211170526
45166CB00005B/1839

* 9 7 8 1 5 2 1 7 3 1 1 5 4 *